Learning to Speak Zucchini

Lessons & Meditations from the Vegetable Garden

ROBERT H. POPE

ABINGDON PRESS
Nashville

LEARNING TO SPEAK ZUCCHINI

LESSONS AND MEDITATIONS FROM THE VEGETABLE GARDEN

Copyright © 1988 by Abingdon Press
All rights reserved.

No part of this work may be reproduced or transmitted in any form or by any means, electronic or mechanical, including photocopying and recording, or by any information storage or retrieval system, except as may be expressly permitted by the 1976 Copyright Act or in writing from the publisher. Requests for permission should be addressed in writing to Abingdon Press, 201 Eighth Avenue South, Nashville, TN 37202.

This book is printed on acid-free paper.

Library of Congress Cataloging-in-Publication Data
POPE, ROBERT H.
  Learning to speak zucchini.
  1. Meditations. 2. Vegetable gardening—Meditations.
I. Title.
BV4832.2.P598   1988   242   87-17489
ISBN 0-687-21332-0
(alk. paper)

Scripture quotations in this publication unless otherwise noted are from the Revised Standard Version of the Bible, copyrighted 1946, 1952, © 1971, 1973 by the Division of Christian Education of the National Council of the Churches of Christ in the U.S.A., and are used by permission.

The Scripture quotation noted KJV (p. 101) is from the King James Version of the Bible.

The Scripture quotation noted NEB (p. 109) is from the New English Bible. Copyright © the Delegates of the Oxford University Press and the Syndics of the Cambridge University Press 1961, 1970. Reprinted by permission.

MANUFACTURED BY THE PARTHENON PRESS AT
NASHVILLE, TENNESSEE, UNITED STATES OF AMERICA

CONTENTS

1. SPEAKING ZUCCHINI WITH HUMILITY ———— 9
   "From the fig tree learn its lesson"—Matthew 24:32

2. THE BATTLE FOR LIFE ———— 20
   "Fight the good fight"—I Timothy 6:12

3. SURVIVAL LANGUAGE ———— 33
   "Blessed are the meek"—Matthew 5:5

4. LOVE IT OR LEAVE IT ———— 45
   "That a man lay down his life for his friends"—John 15:13

5. ABUNDANCE AND EXTRAVAGANCE ———— 58
   "My cup overflows"—Psalm 23:5

6. BREAD FOR THE WORLD ———— 70
   "If a brother or sister is . . . in lack of daily food"—James 2:15

7. WINTER ———— 82
   "Thou hast made summer and winter"—Psalm 74:17

8. THE PARABLE OF THE SOILS ———— 97
   "A sower went out to sow"—Matthew 13:3

*T*he heavens are telling the glory of God;
　　and the firmament proclaims his handiwork.
Day to day pours forth speech,
　　and night to night declares knowledge.
There is no speech, nor are there words;
　　their voice is not heard;
yet their voice goes out through all the earth,
　　and their words to the end of the world.

　　　　　　　　　　　　　　　Psalm 19:1-4

1

SPEAKING ZUCCHINI WITH HUMILITY

From the fig tree learn its lesson. —*Matthew* 24:32

Zucchini is one of the easiest vegetables to grow. You dig the ground. Gather the soil up into a little hill. Scatter four to five seeds across the top and with your fingers poke them about an inch into the soil. In a week's time green appears and begins to increase marvelously and wildly into a vast shrub.

If you have never gardened for vegetables before, zucchini squash is a good one to start with if you are a person who needs immediate success to keep up your interest. It gives you nearly instant encouragement and abundant satisfaction. You even begin to feel a brief sense of power, having created something so lush, useful, and prolific. Soon the vine produces remarkably beautiful yellow blossoms with male and female characteristics (a mini-Eden it seems: new life, sex, with no enemies). Fruit quickly emerges from the end of the female blossom. Without noticing the passing of time, you rapidly find yourself madly searching for people who like squash in order to hold the fecund green invasion in check. If you should overlook a squash hidden beneath the lush vine, you soon discover that an explosive growth has taken place in the garden. Behold, a vegetable as big as your thigh shocks your senses. The temptation will be to parade it about the neighborhood, threatening the kids with this green shillelagh, or to brag about your horticultural skills. *Don't,* because soon comes the fall from grace. The real world makes itself evident. It is not as easy as it had first seemed. Eden has been misunderstood again.

One bright morning as you breathe in the luxuriant beauty of your creation—the vegetable patch, your niche of abundance, which has given you some self-confidence and a feeling that life is not quite so tenuous as you thought— as you look at the vine that has done so well for you, the pit of your stomach suffers a twisting apprehension, the zucchini is anything but healthy. Thirst is the first thought that enters your head. *Has it been that long since the last rain?* You run for the bucket and nearly drown the plant with a torrent of water, yet the next day the illness seems progressive. The lushness has evaporated, the leaves look like you feel some mornings when you have a head cold and are rising to face a tough day. Energy is gone. Life drained, there is a penetrating drudgery to getting up before the sun. Somehow, creation has rebelled against health and fertility.

Each day the plant loses the battle for life. You feel impotent now, when a short time ago there was reason for pride accompanied by quivers of invincibility. When you thought, *How lucky the squash is to have me. It owes its life to me. It came into being because I dug the soil, weeded, cultivated, watered.* Now there is something else the plant needs that you have overlooked or do not know about. All your thoughtfulness, your skills, and your energies have produced a flash in the pan. Now even the vines that seem to be surviving are producing less and the fruit is small and misshapen. You sense defeat and reevaluate your dream.

The first lesson in gardening—and everywhere for that matter—begins to emerge. Life does not easily respond to arrogant, facile solutions. Vitality demands a certain humility. Growth is a learning experience requiring teachable students. It requires us to become conversant with the portions and bits of existence as we receive them—including the corners of our gardens that have been given to us to oversee. Even to allow a variety of squash to grow, we need to learn to speak zucchini. To ask of it, What do you demand of us in order to be alive and healthy and verdant? Growth comes when we attend to all the conditions the plant imposes on us. Speaking zucchini means being willing to satisfy all the terms and articles and clauses in the contract for life abundant.

The dreadfully sagging vine tells of beast and pestilence. You discover the evildoer to be a borer that has wormed its way into the stem just at ground level and is sucking the life out of the center of the stalk. Checking the garden encyclopedias, you begin to learn the language. Spray at the base of the plant with Diazinon if you are not frightened by environmental theories. Otherwise, slice along the length of the stalk until you find the transgressor, then root it out and destroy the wretch. Cover the wound with fresh earth and hope you have learned this much of the language in time. Further checking sends you for the soil test kit. Zucchini likes a soil between 6.5 and 6.8 pH and a good amount of phosphorus to keep blossom end rot in check. Next year you will communicate better with 5-10-5 fertilizer and agricultural limestone. And, a curious dialect emerges—allowing the fruit to mature sends the message to the vine that its work is done, so production slows; to insure productivity until frost keep the green abundance picked at a tender six inches. You become the plant's servant, you become conversant about its loves and hates, what it thrives on, what gives it life and health, what will keep predators and enemies from its door. You are learning to speak zucchini.

It is said that American Indians lived in Pennsylvania hills for thousands of years over the richest veins of coal in the world, never aware of the fire and warmth and power the fossil remains were capable of. It took millions of years to form the fuel, and a million years for humankind to learn the language and begin to stoke their hearths with black chunks of energy. We learn to communicate with things slowly, and who knows how well we are speaking the language right now? We may be like Newton felt, merely playing in the sand on the shore of a vast ocean of the unknown with most of its terms and conditions still not part of our mother tongue. Are we still in the backwater of knowledge, issuing grunts and groans over our universe? Are there other planets somewhere with creatures who, because they speak freely with the cosmos, skate from star to star by some magic we haven't learned as yet?

What makes life abundant? A soil test kit? Warmth in the winter? The Salk vaccine and diet pills? While gardeners learn to speak zucchini, others are putting words to their trade as well. The physician is a language learner. He knows the language called health. He remains teachable about body symptoms and learns to supply what makes tissues and organs do what they were meant to do. Those who implanted Barney Clark's artificial heart are learning to speak the cardiac dialect—maybe at Barney's expense but to someone else's benefit. Wilbur and Orville learned to form the first few syllables of sailing on the wind. They, and later aerodynamicists, spoke to the compressible fluid of the atmosphere with airfoil and wing so that it could answer back with vacuum, lift, and flight. The greatest speaker of the language of life according to Christians was Jesus, who is so good at it he is called by the very basic elements of language—the Word. The metaphor fits. Was Jesus in touch with the language better than anyone before or since? Did he know how to communicate so life became abundant indeed? Did he speak a spiritual tongue that reached beyond the flimsy of material and concrete speech? Was he so in touch with the Author that he knew the words that would lead any listener who took them to heart toward Paul's list of spiritual achievements—love, joy, peace, patience, kindness, goodness, faithfulness, gentleness, self-control (Gal. 5:22-23)? Was he the tangible Word we needed to put shape on the often elusive spiritual dimension? Is the Christian life to be spent learning to speak Jesus? He *is* the Word of Life.

Yet there are dangers in learning the Word. We can take the language and use it as if it were our own. When we learn to speak zucchini will we use the knowledge exclusively to gorge ourselves on its produce? Will we use food as a weapon, or for the world?

So too with life language. If we learn the language well enough, is it possible to use even that wisdom for our own purposes? It is easy to think God will work for us if we speak the proper language; just as we make our gardens work for us when we speak the right language to seed and soil. The gift of language gives us a sense of immense superority because it can be used in a Godlike way, to control events and people.

Is it possible the learner's intent becomes the razor's edge between the holy and unholy? It is like Judas joining the Word followers to make things work for him. When the Kingdom wasn't to be realized on his terms, in self-righteous indignation he betrayed what he thought to be his misguided Teacher. Manipulating God, using for our own purposes the insight, gifts, and authority he has given us: Therein works the demonic brooding of hubris and greed. Even in the sincerest meditation the shadow almost comes without being noticed. "Treat me as the apple of your eye because I am here in prayer while others are mostly about their own business."

Odd how close they are: God and the demonic. Luke reports that Jesus "full of the Holy Spirit" encountered the devil in the wilderness. The Bible describes Satan as a fallen angel. One tiny step separates righteousness from self-righteousness, zeal for God from lust for power, "blessed assurance" from arrogant superiority.

When we learn the langauge of life what will that do for us? Make us authorities on God? Will it give us power to use peoples' guilts and threaten them with their own poor perceptions of themselves? Will we assume the power of the Word? If we used the language for all the selfish purposes that lurk within us, would we really have learned the language at all? Clearly, learning the Word requires of us a certain teachableness. Even zucchini demands some humility. In our gardens we remain the servant, never the Creator. We can hardly tell zucchini how to grow. If we have a compost heap full of nicely decayed leaves with a pH of 4, all the stiff-necked lordly caring in the world will not make zucchini grow when we stubbornly work anything that acidic into the soil. Even with people, little success in relationships results when we approach them as if we knew the very best for them. So too with the language of life.

It is possible to learn a kind of pidgin tongue, a slang, a

mixture of words that speak intermittently of unselfishness, generosity, and kindness between all the really self-centered things we do. Psychologists tell us, for instance, that altruism is not entirely selfless. It rarely comes in an unadulterated form. Altruists, for instance, may act the way they do to feel good about themselves or to get themselves out of a mild depression. Nothing does more for our self-esteem than a feeling of being needed and appreciated.

There is the tale of the man traveling in rural Oklahoma who ran out of gas. He went to a nearby farmhouse to call a service station, but the farmer insisted on taking him to town, bringing him back, and even staying with him until the car was running again. The motorist offered the farmer $10 for his troubles. The altruist adamantly refused; in truth, telling the insistent man with the money, "Look mister, I feel very good about helping you. If I took your money, you'd buy that feeling back from me. And it's not for sale!" So, the language of selflessness, or any other word of life, may not be exactly the King's English. We may hear the authentic word briefly spoken in the strangest way and circumstances.

There is, in a nursing home, a gray misshapen soul who if you get too close smells like she needs a change of diapers; she knows the language. No reason to know it. Surrounded by bed pans, urine-soaked shoes, walkers, roaming victims of frozen arteries telling stories from a world of dreams, the language you'd expect would be foul with oaths. "Curse God and die," would be the best advice in a place where death is a friend. Yet this speaker of life when asked one inch from her ear, How are you today? goes on about her pains and discomforts. Surprising the questioner with her wit, she tells exactly about her lonely day, the uninteresting food, the male nurse who a little carelessly moved her from the bed to the wheelchair that morning. Until suddenly, without anyone expecting it, she grasps the hand of her inquirer and with all the conviction of a lifetime of learning the language blurts out almost as if fearing there might be some misunderstanding, "But God has been good to me!" The language has a certain clarity and truth when spoken under such circumstances. No arrogant superiority there. She wanted no wrong interpretation of her surroundings. Even in a nursing home the word comes at us with paradoxical authenticity. Learning to speak the word of life requires a certain novitiate, subservience, risk, patience, insistence in the face of all the frequent contradictions and unhappy bewilderments. Learning the language is to allow it first to speak to us. It means being very good listeners. We need to listen to our gardens grow if we expect abundance.

A man in New Jersey listens to gardens. It got him in trouble at least once. He will drive miles out of his way if he hears of a backyard vegetable bed. It isn't because he's nosy. He calls it the greening of his soul. He claims that every so often he needs to experience the silence of growth as if to pop a few vitamins to counteract the lack of nourishment in the balance of his life. He sits by gardens and says to himself and anyone who may be listening, "O rich earth, how do you speak to me? Life is possible? Do not be afraid? I thrive in spite of weed and worms and storm?" And he asks, "Do you say life is tenacious? What do you say to me? Except for the gardener I'd grow dandelions and grass? I say back, thank you for giving me your verdant life because I've sweated among your leaves and stalks."

He likes it best when he doesn't meet the gardener personally. He says just seeing the orderliness of the rows, the logic of the companionships between varieties, the method used to stake up the tomatoes, the measure of darkness of the earth, tells him about the caretaker. Much of life is that way, he would say. Just by looking and listening you can learn much about the Caretaker. Yogi Berra wasn't too far off when he said "You can observe a lot just by watching." A person's house, garden, backyard tells you something about the owner. Still, a woman in Piscataway saw this man get out of his car to look and called the police. (It was after this he preferred not to meet the gardeners personally.) When he told them what he was doing they became more suspicious, until he convinced them he was harmless by showing his Patrolman's Benevolent Card thanking him for his donation, signed by his local police chief.

Anyhow, there is something to be said for the silence of gardens and of God. Credit has to be given to those who persist in meeting the silence. Most people get darned uncomfortable with the quiet; antsy if they have nothing to do. Even in our prayers we fill voids and our minds roam to a hundred divergencies, yet after practicing garden watching for a time, the silence becomes a friend you can't do without. In the silence there is warmth, welcome, the merging of Creator and creature, the greening of the soul!

Isaiah's greening touches something within all of us. The strange power that strikes us from his lines, "The mountains and the hills before you shall break forth into singing, and all the trees of the field shall clap their hands" (Isa. 55:12), is the interruption of silence by muted surroundings. It is most of all the quiet things that speak to us most profoundly. These are Isaiah's "sounds of silence," and they are poignant because we too, if we listen carefully and long enough, will hear the same cadences of "peace and joy" of which he so eloquently speaks. Isaiah learned to prepare the soil of his soul in order to let the Lord bring lush verdant sounds out of the barren Judain wastes. We too, if we listen to our gardens speak.

Gardening Note

A dog could be surrounded by cases of canned dog food and starve to death because the cans were not open. In a similar way gardens too can be filled with the foods needed to grow things—nitrogen, phosphorus, potash, as well as trace elements of zinc, iron, copper, and manganese—and still not be able to feed the seed or the sprout with what it needs because the can is not opened, so to speak. The can opener that releases all these nutrients to the soil has to do with the pH condition of the soil. Now this may be as obvious to the home gardener as it is that the earth is shaped like a pear, but it is nonetheless the key to a bountiful harvest. The vegetable garden needs a pH somewhere between 6 and 6.8 to enable it to release food to the plants.

If this business of pH sounds much too clinical, don't be put off by it. Some scientists dreamed up a scale that measures the sourness (acidity) or sweetness (alkalinity) of things. That scale runs from acid to alkaline (0 to 14), with 7 at neutral. Below 7 things need a good dose of antacid; above, they need a little tomato juice to give them mid-course correction. Soils—like humans—mostly complain of too much acid, so they need agricultural limestone spread on them, preferably in the fall. Limestone moves the pH upward on the scale. Aluminum sulfate moves it down toward acidity.

Fortunately, most states have an agricultural agency or

college where you can send soil samples in order to know where your particular patch lies on the scale, and you can add the ingredient needed in order to make your own Garden of Eden. Or, a small soil test kit can be purchased at the local gardening center, and you can test your own samples. If you want to raise the pH one unit, add approximately 2½ pounds of ground limestone to every 100 square feet of soil. If you want to lower it a unit, add 2½ pounds of aluminum sulfate to 100 square feet. Once you get the pH right and you add the humus, compost, and fertilizer, you should step aside before you are knocked down by growing things.

2

THE BATTLE FOR LIFE

Fight the good fight.   —I Timothy 6:12

May and June top the list for gardening. No bugs, weeds, or disease. If the soil is right you can plant, grow, and harvest strawberries, peas, lettuce, radishes, and a few other fast-growing hardy greens. July and August require a different game plan. Weeds emerge overnight. Planting things like beets and carrots in late June requires immense patience since each row bears tiny bits of grass and other unwanted growth. Every emerging beet or carrot stem must be delicately separated from the tares. Bugs descend on the vegetation like a swarm of ants at a sidewalk convention. If not a strict environmentalist, the gardener will begin routinely spraying the tomatoes, beans, squash, turnips, cabbage. If organic by nature, home remedies will be brewed to fight off the invader. Either way the war needs to be fought with a relentless determination. It becomes a matter of survival. Disease too begins to touch a prized vine and fruit: blossom-end rot, verticillium wilt, club root, leaf blight. Not much to do here except to take note to rotate the crops next year to other less infected areas of the garden. Sometimes sprays will help, but the battle rages. One man's solution was to surround his garden with a chicken wire fence, a row of marigolds, and a border of garlic. Half joking he said the fence was to keep out the varmints and dogs, the marigolds the bugs, and the garlic the diseases and evil spirits. Every gardener has a battle on hand.

For every Christian too, the fight seems to be a never ending one. One man greeted his friends as he met them during the day with the salutation, "How goes the battle?" So, even for this believer, faith plays a moving part in the conviction that triumph over the enemy is as ensured as the Easter hymn proclaims: "The strife is o'er the battle done; The victory of life is won; / The song of triumph has begun. Alleluia."[1] Gardening also takes a whole lot of trust, faith, and imagination in the face of the foe to cling to the notion of victory.

Probably the most formidable enemy for the gardener is the woodchuck. This rodent can reduce any small gardener to desperation. It is said about wars that if you have any hope of winning, you have to develop a healthy respect for your enemy. Frustration might not be too strong an emotion either; frustration at the woodchuck's cunning, perseverance, daring, and his insatiable eating habits. A woodchuck, or groundhog, whichever you prefer, will generally mind his own business until by luck (it depends on your point of view of course) he happens to stumble on a paradise some gentleman farmer has sweated over and planted just for him. After the discovery there is no turning him back. He will attack the defenses in broad daylight. Like Rambo heading for the enemy bunker, his heroism takes on a comic insanity. Comic because of his passion and frenzy in the midst of Eden like a little boy in a toy store at Christmas, and insanity because a guy could get killed doing what he is doing.

Still, the odds *are* in favor of the woodchuck. One

desperate farmer tried nearly everything. Someone told him to lay two feet of black plastic around the garden; the animal wouldn't cross it. Not so with this brazen beast. Another told him to plant a fence; that is, bury the wire six inches underground. But a desperately hungry woodchuck will either go over it or burrow under it if he has the time. Another cure: Find his hole and throw in a smoke grenade just made for such dastardly beasts. The trouble with this is that the critter has designed an ingenious labyrinth of tunnels and exits, some camouflaged beyond discovery. An electric fence. Now there's an idea. One man put up a fence and his dog's tail hit it once—just once—and he wouldn't go within twenty feet of the garden if there had been a sizzling sirloin waiting for him at the firing line. But not the groundhog. Almost without noticing it he brushes past the shock. When you are about to enter the most sensuously palatable wonderland you ever saw, it hardly seems bothersome at all to notice a bolt out of the blue. After trying all of the above, one gardener, who took great pride in his Christian pacifism, borrowed a .22 caliber rifle from his neighbor concluding that lead poisoning was the only hope for his garden. With the strains of "The strife is o'er, the battle done" ringing in his head, he set out to do what he swore he would never do again—use a firearm. But the woodchuck must have been smarter than even he could have predicted because he never came back, saving his own hide and the farmer's principles. Actually he probably didn't come back because he'd already cleaned out the place. Rabbits will leave something for the gardener, groundhogs conquer a garden as if it were attacked by a power mower.

Gardening seems to check out with every other aspect of life in that the enemy is often formidable. In the garden, it is nature against itself. For the rest, much of the heartache is man against himself. Part of learning the language in either case is to know how to help nature or oneself work for the good. I suppose it may come as a shock to some that nature (or oneself) isn't necessarily good. After the Mount St. Helen's disaster, a Sierra Club spokesperson criticized the restoration planned for certain areas of the mountain. If nature did it, it should not be disturbed but let alone to work out its own salvation. We are not to disagree with Mother Nature, since all that she does is somehow for the best. This is a theory that rings true to the nature foods craze. Natural-food stores shelve their products in the same sterile factory-produced packages found in supermarkets. Health food is big business, and it makes money mostly because people believe that if it's natural it's good for you. Which is better? Natural butter from "organic" cows or margarine with its long list of chemicals on the carton? Probably better to use neither one.

All this tempts us, of course, to identify God with nature. We attempt to prove God's grandeur by nature's awe. Even the words to our hymns elevate nature to high places—as if becoming like nature is the ultimate goal in life.

> Like thy springs and running waters
> Make me crystal pure;
> Like thy rocks of towering grandeur
> Make me strong and sure.
> Like thy dancing waves in sunlight
> Make me glad and free;
> Like the straightness of the pine trees
> Let me upright be.
> Like the arching of the heavens
> Lift my thoughts above.[2]

We forget that our streams run through our land filled with cancer-producing chemicals and enough tires, bottles, and beer cans to fill Yankee Stadium. We forget that rocks of towering grandeur occasionally explode with incredible violence. We forget the ocean waves as a sometime villain that washes away homes and shorelines and ships at sea. We forget that the pine to admire is the one with a greater instinct for beauty, the one that clings to a cliff with its twisted frame as if wired to life at the barren crest of a mountain peak. We forget that the arching heavens are quite inhospitable to life. The vast cosmos is a silent, deadly place.

Nature can be horribly cruel. Annie Dillard testifies to the terror and injustice of the insect world when she writes, "The Creator is no puritan. A creature [parasite] need not work for a living, creatures simply steal and suck and be blessed for all that with a share—an enormous share—of sunlight and air."[3] Nature can be not only mysteriously one-sided, it can also be violent, destructive, horribly dull, indifferent, and sinister. So if gardening helps us at all to learn the language of life, it should certainly help us see that nature rages against itself. Paul writes, "We know that the whole creation has been groaning in travail . . . not only the creation, but we ourselves" (Rom. 8:22-23). A brokenness, a flaw exists in nature and human nature. No one should know that or see that more clearly than the Christian gardener. Both nature and humankind need redemption. Natural man, too, rages against himself.

A story from *The New York Times* makes the point. The condor is an endangered species of bird; only about thirty remain in the world. Ornithologists have been trying desperately to reverse the trend toward the demise of the condor, so a team of experts watched from half a mile away the only egg known to have been laid in the season. According to this article, preserving the species is a little like trying to reform the unrepentant. Aghast, the watchers saw the egg crash to the rocks below. "Its parents, fighting over whose turn it was to sit, had knocked it out of the nest. So far, despite a million-dollar project to preserve the birds by learning more about their habits, the California condor has eschewed salvation. And will probably continue to do so—unless it stops behaving like a human being and starts acting like a bird." So, both man and beast groaneth in travail.

What is the reason for the travail? Does the near fatal (or fatal) flaw defy description, an explanation? Scientists wring their hands and hope for a turning point in natural man's tendency to self-destruct. Carl Sagan writes: "From an extraterrestrial perspective, our global civilization is clearly on the edge of failure in the most important task it faces: to preserve the lives and well-being of the citizens of the planet. Should we not be willing to explore vigorously, in every nation, major changes in the traditional ways of doing things . . .?"[4] And the poet agonizes over the paradox of his own behavior:

> And pray to God to have mercy on us
> And pray that I may forget
> These matters that with myself I too much discuss
> Too much explain
> Because I do not hope to turn again
> Let these words answer
> For what is done, not to be done again
> May the judgment not be too heavy on us.[5]

And the Bible, as is its character, pulls no punches, saying, "The heart is deceitful above all things, and desperately corrupt; who can understand it?" (Jer. 17:9). And the religious put names to it: pride, lust, gluttony, selfishness, sloth, jealousy, violence. But the mystery of the flaw remains except for this hint or bit of evidence witnessed by garden watchers. A war is going on, a civil war within nature and humankind. We are out to self-destruct. Richard Nixon's greatest sin, the one that evoked the subtlest outrage, was that he didn't get rid of the tapes *before* they became lethal. He touched the basic flaw—he was his own worst enemy—and we didn't like it because it touched something deep in most of us. The alcoholic will not stop even when seeing life dissolving in a vast nightmare of drunken horrors. The selfish man will not stop his frenzied accumulation of wealth even though he knows he becomes more isolated and estranged and out of touch with the largest share of humanity with each new million he adds to his accounts. The woman whose husand is unfaithful refuses to stop eating, her obesity giving her reasons for his rejection and her failure as a woman, and thus adding the final, inevitable conclusion to the marriage. An older man faced with cancer and death is visited in the hospital by a minister he doesn't know. The pastor says, not wishing to offend his religious principles or prejudices, "If you'd like, I would be privileged to pray with you."

"No," says the departing man. "I would feel it would be quite unnecessary now." Why would he not enlist all the resources he could possibly find to give him strength? Why would he deliberately die in his sins?

If there is any lingering doubt about the battle, clearly the war rages the loudest and is most evident when the highest good emerges. Gardens that seem like paradise, perfect in beauty or yielding the most abundant produce, have required the greatest vigilance. A Gandhi, a King, their selflessness soaring above even the best of us, turn people violently against them. And the cross towers in human history as the affirmation of the self-destructive forces that lie at the center of the human heart.

Any serious meditation on the cross leaves us with blood on our hands, and we wonder how it could have happened. But we cannot help ourselves; we are addicts under a compulsion by our own inventions to deny, ignore, reason away, or, by whatever means occurs to us, crucify the very gifts we've been given that are our best hope for real living. We not only crucify Christ, we so often, to our horror, find ourselves crucifying the best in us or misusing the best in us, in ways that cause us to self-destruct.

Fearful that generosity will lead us to financial hardship, we tighten our grip on our possessions until they become so important to us we cannot bear the thought of separating ourselves from them. We *become* our possessions and lose our humanity.

Doubting the wisdom of kindness or gentleness in a world of intense competition, we too become intimidators. Living by aggression we believe that our survival depends on being among the world's winners. We fear being too good; we'll get run over by the takers! So we crucify that part of us that would make us into the best of human beings, and we pat ourselves on the back for our successes even while experiencing an unexplainable emptiness within.

Distrusting people, even those who we find by biological circumstances are part of the family, we keep our distance. We hesitate with our affections, hold our feelings close to ourselves suspecting they might be somehow used against us. We cut off the really supporting and encouraging experiences everyone needs to enable him or her to have the courage to grow into a whole and mature human being. Whoever said it, is right—in this nuclear age, almost exclusively by our own doing, *we* are an endangered species (along with the condor).

While all this confessing about our addiction to self-destruction may seem a depressing preoccupation, it is not. The only hope for eventual victory is to know the enemy; and in the words of *Pogo's* Porky Pine, "It is us." At one zoo the sign over one of the viewing windows in the great apes pavilion reads, "The most vicious animals in the world." As you peer in, you are shocked to see your own likeness reflected back at you by a mirror. The hope for a victory over the enemy lies in our recognizing him, taking him into account, and making plans for the battle. J. R. R. Tolkien wrote, "It does not do to leave a dragon out of your calculation, if you live near him." Victory will not be ours until we see clearly just how close the habitations of dragons are to us, and since this is a fight against the darkness that "already" resides within us, the obvious conclusion is that we will not win by our own ingenuity, cleverness, or self-analysis. "Every kingdom divided against itself is laid waste," said Jesus. Because we know only too well what Jesus says is true, we will outwit even our most courageous attempts to implicate ourselves. We will not allow ourselves to look too long into the mirror. We will quickly get very nervous and madly look around for someone else to blame, or we will lull ourselves into believing we live in an O.K. world. The grass in our yards is green and carefully clipped and the azaleas are brilliant and our streets are safe. The fight is elsewhere. In the city, in the desert in Iran, in the mountains in Lebanon, in the Pentagon, but not here. We have no battle to wage. Yet how many times have we prayed Jesus' prayer without giving it a thought, saying, "Deliver us from evil." What evil? Deliver us from a selfishness that finds no time for even those we claim to love. Deliver us from the callousness of impatience with old people. Deliver us from taking our nation and its politics lightly. Deliver us from indifference. Deliver us from thinking we're O.K. with God as long as we mind our own business. Deliver us from believing we're Christian enough without a commitment to Christ that requires daily praise and prayer and witness to his benefits. Deliver us from believing we can make it without God's help.

The only hope of victory comes to us as we contemplate the cross. As we do, it is the mirror in which we see our own image, a deadly and divine image. An image of tragedy and victory. An image of defeat and triumph. The defeat is our own, the triumph is that all that is holy in our midst will prevail in the end. Through all the self-serving, all the pettiness, all the nasty little bits of envy and prejudice and superiority, all the backbiting, we have a hope of victory because at the cross God towered above all in a magnificent proclamation of grace. The symbol and hope of victory is the cross.

During World War II, even during the darkest days following Pearl Harbor, most Americans maintained a faith in the final victory by the Allied powers, even though they knew great sacrifices lay ahead of them. In those bleak times when most people had an A on their windshield allowing them the minimum ration of gasoline and had in their pockets or purse a book of coupons allowing them to buy a couple of pounds of beef a week if they could afford it, confidence in that victory was encouraged by the beginning of many backyard gardens. These became known as "Victory Gardens." Raising your own food enhanced the war effort by releasing agricultural workers to the more essential armament industry. But, most of all, these gardens proclaimed a faith in the future. The planting of every seed was a proclamation that we would still be around as a free people to enjoy the harvest! Those gardens became a symbol of triumph as, in a sense, they do today, because for the gardener they represent a conviction that the victory will be won over all the destructive elements that would turn that backyard patch of ground into a nonproductive, weed-filled grassland. So too the cross remains forever embedded in the ground of our being as one final triumph over all that would destroy us.

Like nature, we rage against ourselves. The enemy is formidable. So is the Victor. Believing in him and "fighting the good fight" remains forever our only hope.

Gardening Note

"O Lord . . . . If there is pestilence or blight or mildew or locust or caterpillar . . . whatever prayer, whatever supplication is made by any man . . . hear you in heaven . . . and act" (I Kings 8:37-39).

Prayer, of course, is one way to fight any battle, but if you want to throw your own actions after your garden-variety prayers, there is organic home brew, insecticide, a fence, companion planting, bug picking by hand, electricity, garter snakes, and toads, all of which can be enlisted in the fight against bug, beast, and pestilence.

But there are certain tricks of the trade too. For instance, one gardener confessed that he had given up growing cabbage. Every time he tried it he lost the battle to root maggots and cabbage worm. He would set out a beautiful cabbage seedling carefully started indoors in March. It would be the picture of health—that dull bluish-green silky leaf seemed almost impervious to any enemy. But after almost leaping out of the soil in the first few weeks, something stopped it dead in its tracks. Growth stalled. Leaf wilted. Stalk drooped. The beautiful green turned to sick yellow. The problem? Tiny black flies had laid eggs at the base of the stem or in the earth surrounding it. These eggs hatched into worms, which feverishly worked their way to the root where they ate away the life of the plant. The cure?

There is a remedy, which could be apocryphal, yet desperation can lead to nearly any radical act. One man, it is said, recognized the problem and removed all twelve of his wilting cabbages, washed off the roots, replaced the soil that had been around each plant with good, rich, fresh humus, which had been given a dose of Diazinon, replanted his stalks, and they eventually grew into mature cabbages before frost. Possibly, if you are not afraid to admit defeat, a better idea would be to buy the mature heads of cabbage at the farm stand for *that* year at least.

Yet there is an almost infallible prevention if you act as you set the seedlings out. Simply make a mat and slip it around the plant stem. The mat prevents the fly from laying its eggs. This can be made from tar paper, black plastic, or old newspaper. Just cut a piece about six inches square; from the midpoint of one side of the square, make a slit to the center of the square and slip it around the stem of the plant, putting a little dirt on the edges to hold it down. That's all. No maggots.

The other danger to cabbage comes from a green worm that by the miracle of adaptation perfectly matches the leaf color of the plant. He eats Swiss-cheese patterns in the foliage, and if allowed to satisfy himself, he will strip the stalk bare and kill the plant. But this almost invisible caterpillar can be controlled by a spray. If you are

suspicious of sprays, this one shouldn't stimulate any of your fears of toxic poisoning. It's a nontoxic, nonchemical called Bacillus thüringiensis. Just spray as directed every seven to ten days. No cabbage worms.
Still one small trick, even for this simple cure. Cabbage has a waxy leaf. Water doesn't adhere, it runs off. Bacillus thüringiensis will also. Just put a few drops of household dish detergent in the spray and it will nicely coat every leaf—and then victory at last; you can eat cole slaw with every summer hot dog.

3

SURVIVAL LANGUAGE

Blessed are the meek, for they shall inherit the earth.
—Matthew 5:5

Hildegarde Quimby is a gardener. She is eighty years old. Every morning she pops out her hearing aid "so's not to be disturbed" and makes her way slowly and painfully into the backyard, where she maintains an 8 x 10-foot patch of tomatoes, beans, and squash. She is a sight. A stool placed carefully between the rows supports her so there is no strain on her knees as she weeds or hoes or picks. She wears a bright ruffly housecoat and a broad-brimmed straw hat to keep the sun from "straining her brain," she says. Her face remains quite content as she scratches at the soil at her feet. The furrows and lines that make up her features seem to be a part of her love for growing things—as if God meant to plow her complexion right in with the rows of her garden. The straw mulch she uses nearly matches her hair, which appears in patches from under her bonnet. She seems a fragile, delicate, bright spirit working her piece of the turf in the morning sun as if a rose had been mistakenly planted among the turnips.

Hildegarde has been gardening, she says, since she was six years old when her mother took her to her "patch" every day to plant or weed as the season demanded. She picks up the soil and squeezes it in her hand. It remains in the form she has pressed it into. "If that soil had run out between my fingers, it would have had no growing power." Crumbling the lump of dirt between her palms, she admires the quality of looseness, the lack of clay and therefore the soil's "good drainage." She says, "God made the best soil just like the best people—not running off in all directions, but with holding power when squeezed by things that happen to everyone; yet with good drainage, letting the troubles you can let go of trickle on out of your soul."

Hildegarde seems to represent everything fragile and delicate. She could be blown away by a cough, yet she has a tenacity and toughness of character that has carried her past her eightieth year. She is good for other, less assured persons who need to be reminded of what strength and toughness means. But she is also good for those who live by their machismo, because she is a reminder that all we so often associate with survival—brawn, muscular development, youth, aggressive competitive drive, and virility—have very little to do with tenacity and endurance and spirit and toughness. Delicate Mrs. Quimby can lick them all when it comes to determination, guts, and the will to live without complaint. Besides, she is a gardener and knows about the inspiration one gets from growing things.

There is a story about Hildegarde that carries the essence of her spirit. It seems her daughter, with whom she lived at the time, died rather suddenly. They had been very close, and Hildegarde was overcome with grief. For the first time in anyone's memory, she seemed to give up and lose touch with her vitality. Her son-in-law, who was in the florist business, became so concerned with her depression he took her with him when he made the rounds of the wholesale greenhouses to order his house plants and flowers. He says that he saw a difference in her the day he helped her from the car into the long, narrow runway of the lush, glass-enclosed ocean of flowers. It was early December, and 5,000 square feet of red poinsettias greeted them. Like magic, the torture melted from her in that sea of fire. She never despaired again. She said it was as if that very place were aflame with the glory of God.

But there is a contrast—or it would at least *seem* to be a contrast—between the frail Hildegarde and her love for gardening. In gardens the strong get preferential treatment. The weak and sickly quickly die off or are pulled up to make way for the flourishing and hardy. One gardener says the thing he dislikes the most is thinning out his seedlings. Plantings of carrots or beets eventually force him to pull up more than 70 percent of the young plants before they crowd one another to the point where the root crop cannot develop. He says he imagines himself a diabolical god who coldly decides who will live and who will die. He selects his victims by their feebleness and position. "Ah, there is a group of fragile stems next to that towering strength; I shall just rid the earth of such weakness" . . . then he thinks, "God help me! I sound as if I am some unaffected monster ridding the world of the infirm, the retarded, the disabled." So, he says he often deliberately pulls up the best and leaves the feeble, hoping they will develop, given a chance, into a respectable crop.

In nature, the fittest survive, or so the theory goes. Yet in life language, we hear, "Blessed are the *meek*, for they shall inherit the earth." One wonders about this perplexity; credulity lies in which camp? Nearly everything we experience seems to favor the fit. Those who inherit popularity, financial success, power and authority over others, and superiority in the marketplace appear to be the strong, the confident, the proud, the aggressors, the noisy, the intimidators. Meek appears to mean setting your sights for less, being satisfied with second place, coming to terms with mediocrity, losing much of your share of the good life. We have become accustomed to winning by coercion through stimulating latent fears in the unsuspecting and timid. Our society seems to have very few models of success by means of caring, feeling for, or support for one another. In fact, very often we distrust those too quick with praise, overt consideration, or easily expressed feelings. What indeed are we to make of Jesus' extravagant claim for the meek—the gentle in spirit? We must ask, would Jesus survive the marketplace? Paul Scherer tells of the businessman who pursues the same thought: "What would happen to me if I tried to carry on my business as Christ would want me to do it? I'd be ruined!" The answer comes with blunt realism: "And what will happen to you if you don't? What kind of ruin do you want?"[1] That man clearly had a limited view of survival, even in shop and store. We have to be careful about survival. Survival can mean existence, conformity, breathing in and out. A couple proudly announce, "In thirty years of marriage, we have never had an argument!" If true, one of the two is a nonperson, a mere survivor with no passion, no fire. One can survive though dead for years.

Clearly (if we allow the Spirit to move us), Jesus' meekness comes closer to Hildegarde than it does to timidity, passivity, and failure. The meek make things grow and feed the hungry. The meek listen, study, humble themselves before nature—they learn to speak zucchini—and the earth responds with abundance. So too, do those who allow God to teach them. The learners of life language will inherit (maybe even save) the earth. It will not be the aggressive, the ambitious who do it. Ambition has gotten us nuclear weapons. Ambition keeps their threat lingering over our heads. Ambition has given us the poor and hungry. Ambition has produced apartheid and 226 Protestant denominations in America. Ambition, aggressive virility does *not* survive—at least not without a whole range of harrowing problems. Hildegarde survives. Teachable people survive. Love survives. Love for a pea patch. Love for God. "Love abides."

In spite of the notion it is the "fit" that survive, the garden sometimes surprises. Last year's tomato seed from weakened and rotted, cast-away fruit survives the winter along the garden path and grows courageously into a plant clinging to the poor earth. The broccoli, half eaten by rabbits in the spring, flourishes, with a little care, producing a stalk for picking. Even in death, the ultimate failure, bean and pea vines cast into a pile will compost into black richness that brings life to a garden. It is not *always* the strong who make it.

Yet much of our world is Darwinian by conviction. The perception that the aggressive win is everywhere. From sports to politics to business to church, the macho spirit is synonymous with success. Football, the most dangerous of games, sends more than 400,000 players to emergency rooms each year with all kinds of injuries from sprains to broken necks, yet the game is revered in America. Clergy regularly pray over the local team invoking God to bless the athletes with the winning spirit. Our top politician, the president, gets elected more by his self-confident image, his will to win, his ability to overwhelm the competition and manipulate others by his success than by his ability to govern. He needs to prove he's a winner, or other than joining the tourist line he'll never see the inside of the White House. In business the competition is so tough it has produced the "Type-A" personality with its heart attacks, ulcers, alcoholism, a wide variety of family problems, exhaustion, and in more up-to-date terms, "burn out," to say nothing of "mid-life crises." The church, too, following the lead of the secular in its passion for the image of success, issues slogans like "Tough times never last, tough people do," tough people being the equivalent of successful people. It is hard to imagine Jesus being judged by these criteria—aggression, self-centeredness, prestigious success, acquisition of power, survival at all costs, pragmatic judgment, competitiveness. He would fail in all categories, yet we reward most of all those who have all these "attributes." The reflective, idealistic, compassionate, sacrificing, self-denying, sensitive personality that we may admire does not receive the prizes our world is so ready to give its winners. Jesus praised meekness; our world rewards the competitor.

Yet, as a gardener looks over a field and wonders about survival, maybe a hint, a notion of meaning emerges. How have these plants survived? This thick-walled pepper of delicate flavor? This extra-sweet, wilt-resistant corn? This disease-resistant tomato? This burpless cucumber that treats the stomach with some respect? Have all these varieties come to the garden patch through their own virility, strength, superiority, fitness? By natural selection? Or was there an *intervenor*?

The American Indian planted corn and the survival of the earliest settlers depended on it, especially through the severe Massachusetts winters. But as those first immigrants thanked God for the saving grace of the maize, it had to be a feeble crop at best. Disease and pests eating into the harvest diminished the return. The ears often appeared one to a stalk, with areas where kernels had not developed. They were no doubt tough, lacking in flavor. We would judge them unworthy of the boiling pot and table. They could not compare to today's huge ears, golden kernels, rich with sweetness in deep, neat, well-filled rows. The horticulturist and botanist have intervened. The fittest has survived and flourished by evolution *and* by intrusion. Most likely survival has more to do with grace than fitness.

Again, it is the language learner who is the survivor—that is, those who are humble enough to learn the system, those willing enough to be shown. Phytologists don't create new and better tomatoes. They learn the language and, by what they are given and shown, help the plants become more disease-resistant, more succulent, better able to cope with environmental enemies. So too the person open to grace. Even the weakest, the least likely, can become more than a survivor—dare it be said, a winner?

Some of the revolutions being imposed on us for the better have come from those feminists who do not want to be like men but who believe in the quality of the feminine; and from the disabled who desire to enter the mainstream of society. They are teaching those of us who are willing to learn their language that being a woman or being disabled or being mentally retarded does not mean weakness. The feminist does have a message for those who live by their virility—masculinity hasn't necessarily produced a better world. The women at Princeton Seminary once made the point in an amusing way. In a chapel service being held after a discussion on sexist language in religious literature with some of the faculty, Psalm 116 was read responsively. The chapel leader that morning, a woman seminarian, asked the men to read a line, then the women, and so on. The psalm continued in that fashion until it came to verse 11, when it was the women's turn to read: "I said in my consternation, men are all a vain hope." It is reported the psalm was never completed owing to spontaneous laughter.

Nor do the disabled emerge as the weak. The quadriplegic who does daily battle with suppositories, bladder infections, inaccessible buildings and sidewalks and buses, often captures our admiration for his or her perseverance, determination, and ability to accept what he or she has been given. There is nothing weak about driving a car, going to college and earning a degree, finding a job and supporting yourself when spinal cord injury has rendered your limbs nearly useless.

And the mentally retarded show us that tenderness and courage are not incompatible. There is a story of the brain-damaged child who, on seeing a man in a wheelchair in church for the first time, left her seat during the passing of the peace and hugged the disabled worshiper. She caught something of the spirit of the moment, and in her simple genuine concern did what most people would like to have had the courage to do in that public place and in that praiseworthy moment.

From such people the survival language that comes to us is the capacity to accept circumstances we are unable to change, the ability to see ourselves *among* others instead of as the *one* among others, the inclination to see the best instead of the worst, and a faith in the time to come. But these graces, with few exceptions, are mostly learned (or given). Our natural inclinations are otherwise, "So we were by nature children of wrath" (Eph. 2:3). It is our natural inclination to get even, return evil for evil, and distrust one another, but then comes the Intervenor, who helps us take into account the measure of our lostness and suggests to us some of the reasons we remain on the endangered species list.

Certainly winning isn't the only thing. The aphids that suddenly appear on the broccoli stalk like thousands of tiny lice and cover the leaves with their excretions, sometimes become uncontrollable and win. But they also lose when the plant dies. Bacteria too, which kill off their host, win a hollow victory because they cut off their own livelihood. The true winners are the bacteria that can live off their host without killing it. The real winners are those microbes that take into account the necessity of *everyone's* survival. Even modern evolutionists seem to be learning a different language—survival has more to do with cooperation, partnership, and agreement than it does with strength, aggressiveness, ambition, the competitive spirit, winning at all costs. Lewis Thomas, the author-physician, writes,

> A century ago there was a consensus that evolution was a record of open warfare among competing species, that the fittest were the strongest aggressor, and so forth. Now it begins to look different. The great success in evolution, the mutants who have made it, have done so by fitting in with and sustaining the rest of life.
>
> Up to now we might be counted among the brilliant successes, but flashy and perhaps unstable. We should go warily into the future, looking for ways to be more useful, listening more carefully for signals, watching our step and having an eye out for partners.[2]

The Christian answer to survival is also moving into the future by listening more carefully for signals, watching our step, and having an eye out for partners who are willing to learn the life language with us, allowing the

Intervenor to hybridize us into abundant spirits, gift givers, bearers of the abundance of God's love. Survival depends on allowing oneself to be made into something *other* than nature (and natural selection) had in mind. It's preparing oneself to let the Lord grow in the soil of one's own life and existence. It is adapting oneself to the environment of God and preparing oneself for the danger-filled environment that is given to us.

One such practitioner of survival says he is still learning the language that will allow God to graft him onto God's vine. But for the grace of God, he says, he would be a strange mutant—disruptive, morose, hostile, belligerent, self-aggrandizing, offensive. Now, since he has been practicing garden watching, so to speak (the religious term is *contemplation*), he feels his countenance is changing. He is learning a life language that is gradually beautifying his soul. He knows it sounds in itself arrogant to say that, but still he is not the person he was ten or twenty years ago. He has learned to make allowances for others, to laugh a little more often, to live mostly by principle rather than impulse, to at least much of the time resist the desire to get even—allowing the mercy he has already so often received manage the angry moment. Often, he says, in his contemplation the silence *becomes* the Intervenor. There is a brief holiness about it, an air of sacredness; and, like Peter on the mountain witnessing the transfiguration of Christ (Mark 9:5, 6), there arises within him an intense desire to remain in that interlude forever, wishing to build a permanent residence in that stillness. He says because he has come to know the silence he has become a survivor, much better equipped to face darkness or fears that would have formerly paralyzed him. He says he has a much better chance to replace the malice within himself with forgiveness, the despair with hope, the sorrow with joy, the dividing walls between persons with love. He has become God's hybrid—a mixture of what he still is and what God would have him be. He is gradually becoming the meek, and he will someday be one of the inheritors of the earth.

Gardening Note

Sometimes the gardener has to be the intervenor.

Both rabbits and squash have similar reputations. They produce more than seems necessary or reasonable. Noah must have been very careful to invite only one pair of rabbits on the Ark, otherwise he would have needed to acquire a taste for hare stew rather quickly or move himself, Mrs. Noah, and the kids into a dinghy. Zucchini, yellow squash, and a variety of other members of the same family will also overproduce, which is why there are so many cookbooks devoted exclusively to zucchini. But once in a while along comes a year when, in spite of the appearance of blossoms and the generally good health of the vine, no fruit appears.

The problem is too many male and too few female blossoms. (Of course, there also may not be enough pollinating insects around. The most industrious, the bee, succumbs to many modern sprays and often either gets exterminated or driven away.) Male blossoms prefer long days and warm nights; female, the shorter days and cooler nights. So when the vine comes into blossom at mid-summer or thereabout, it will most likely bear a majority of male blossoms. Toward the end of the summer, the balance will change and more females will appear. Fortunately, some overlap occurs, particularly at mid-season. Otherwise life would be dull, indeed!

The gardener can intervene, however, particularly in those years when the weather favors the male. By means of an artist's paintbrush, the gardener can do the fertilizing in order to be sure every female blossom that appears will bear fruit. Simply identify the male blossom, reach inside with the brush and pick up some pollen from the stamen. The female has a swelling which resembles a miniature squash on the stem just at the base of the blossom. (The male, of course, lacks this swelling.) Just scatter a little pollen on the four-part curled pistil inside each female flower on the vine. Actually one male is enough to handle all the females (that, of course, is not a judgment or a sexist statement; just in this case a fact of life). Be sure the male selected is a fully open flower—if it isn't the pollen may not be ripe and the brush will come away clean.

In two or three days your amateur artificial insemination will be determined a success or failure by the development of the swelling at the base of the female flower. If it gradually shrivels away, you should try again. If it expands and begins to grow into a squash, you have succeeded. Soon you will have squash in abundance, and you'd do well to dig out the zucchini cookbooks and get busy in the kitchen.

4

LOVE IT OR LEAVE IT

Greater love has no man than this, that a man lay down his life for his friends. —*John 15:13*

Certain gardening crowds say that plants grow better when you talk to them. They say plants like to be treated as equals. They have feelings and need our affection; sweet words whispered at romantic interludes stimulate growth and make them feel as if they belong. After all, doesn't everyone need to feel needed, cared about, and loved? According to some reports, a group of wildlife preservationists even go further and claim that plants not only have feelings, they have rights as well. There is one such plants' rights group that say you shouldn't mow your lawn, because it has a "sort of consciousness"; it has feelings. The effort is called "save the grass campaign" and has almost six thousand followers. Quite possibly all this is a bit exaggerated, however. After all, who could hear the cries of pain above the roar of a lawn mower? But learning to speak zucchini has nothing to do with the above. Learning zucchini language isn't talking to plants, it is listening to plants; after all, how do you say "I love you" in zucchini?

Still, all these conversationists do have a point. Gardening does have to be something of a love affair if it is ever to rise above drudgery. There is the story of the woman whose husband planted an apple tree, promising her the most wonderful succulent fruit imaginable. Several years later when the tree matured, the poor woman dreaded seeing her husband appear at the kitchen door with bushels of the "succulent fruit." Every fall her kitchen became a large assembly of boiling cauldrons, mason jars, apple mashers, cider jars, and sauce. Once when she found herself at the peak of the season and at the peak of frustration about what *more* she could do with all those apples, her neighbor appeared. In desperation, her hair a mess, her kitchen floor sticky with spilled juice, the counters covered with steaming containers, the woman asked her friend, "What am I ever going to do about all these apples?" Incredible wisdom resounded from her friend's lips: "Marybell, if I were you, I'd go out and chop down that tree!" Well, that's one way to get rid of the strain and burden. Similarly, with gardening, you'd better love it or leave it. The gnats, the sweat running down onto your glasses, bending over the beans to pick a long row and hardly managing to regain an erect bearing because of the pain paralyzing the lumbar region of your spine—all these typical endearments demand no less than a love affair between the gardener and the garden.

Yet not every farmer is in love with the land. For example, in an area that once started out as farmland and now has become suburbia, there are two vast farms completely surrounded by one-family homes, some of which are mansions. As in most suburban communities, property taxes have become incredibly burdensome, mostly owing to soaring costs of schools and services; so the town councils seek ways to keep the taxes on private homes within reason. Therefore, they look for land to bring in attractive office-type corporations, apartments, or luxury villages. Irresistably, Farmer Jones, the owner of one of the two farms, has sold off land to the developers, commercial property running more than $100,000 an acre. He has become a millionaire. Farmer Brown has not sold; he still holds on to his almost priceless land because he is a farmer at heart. A most joyous sight is to see him setting out young peach saplings. His doing so affirms his love affair, affirms his desire to keep the land long into the future as an orchard that produces blossom and fruit in spite of the lure of an easier life counting his money. Farmer Jones, however, has sold nearly everything. He has a vast produce stand where he sells "fresh" vegetables trucked in from somewhere else in the state. He has a complex of stores—liquor, restaurant, meat market, jewelry. He has sold to large hotel chains, corporations, and developers. Farmer Brown has a passion for the luxuriant blossoming sort of green. For him, there is a limit to offices that look like military bunkers or glass cathedrals. He cannot bear seeing his land plastered over with asphalt parking lots. Farmer Brown is a farmer in love with his land. Farmer Jones is a financier, in love with the green of his money. A farmer or gardener needs to be in love with the business of growing things, or it's no go. To make the sacrifice and pain bearable there has to be a deeper motive.

It almost sounds too hackneyed to use that four-letter word *love*. It has come to mean so many superficial things. It can be used, for instance, as a word of admiration: "Oh, I simply love that dress you're wearing." Or, it can be used to mean sex: "O.K., let's make love." Or it can mean inspiration, well-being, good feelings: "I feel like I've just fallen in love again." Or it can denote the score of zero in tennis. But none of these meanings bears up under the hardships any relationship brings. The love necessary for gardeners and in every significant connection we make in life has to bear up under burden, affliction, curse. (After all wasn't Adam's curse that he would work the soil, clearing it of weeds and pests at the sweat of his brow and the pain in his back?)

If a God exists at all, likewise he too must be in love with this vast planetary garden called earth. He has to be in order to keep his patience in the darkness we have inflicted on it. Our misuse of it; the pollution and paving and privation of it; our selfishness with it; hoarding the best, stealing from primitive people, *owning* it; our wars over it; the incessant brutalities in the back streets of Belfast and Beirut, as well as senseless killing over the Falklands, Chad, and Central America. God must be in love; there is no other explanation for his perseverance.

Someone said God has loves, not reasons. So too, when the weeds get ahead because you have been called to do other things, or the beetle destroys your beans, or your cherished and prized cucumber vine is eaten by rodents—you ask, "Why do I do it? Why all the planting, digging, sowing, hoeing, weeding? Do I labor for insect, rabbit, and grass? Why not learn to sip iced tea on the porch and buy at the produce market?" And no reason comes to you. Some other ingredient compels you to the seed and soil. What mighty quality of perseverance might this be except love?

Hosea tells movingly about how God loves. Israel he likens to a harlot whom Hosea takes for his own wife: "And the Lord said to me, 'Go again, love a woman who is beloved of a paramour and is an adulteress; even as the Lord loves the people of Israel, though they turn to other gods and love cakes of raisins' " (Hos. 3:1).

As Hosea's agony over his wife's affairs bears in on him

as a nearly intolerable pain, so too he speculates about God's feelings in his relationships with Israel. By his own firsthand experience, Hosea knows the wounded quandary of God:

> What shall I do with you, O Ephraim?
> What shall I do with you, O Judah?
> Your love is like a morning cloud,
>   like the dew that goes early away. (Hos. 6:4)

Yet, as Hosea still loves his wife, God still loves Israel, and in a marvelous soliloquy God reminds himself who he is:

> How can I give you up, O Ephraim!
>   How can I hand you over, O Israel!
> How can I make you like Admah!
>   How can I treat you like Zeboiim!
> My heart recoils within me,
>   my compassion grows warm and tender.
> I will not execute my fierce anger,
>   I will not again destroy Ephraim;
> *for I am God and not man,*
>   *the Holy One in your midst,*
>   *and I will not come to destroy.*
>   (Hos. 11:8-9, emphasis added)

That thankfully, tells us of the God who loves *in spite of*. In an analogous way, the farmer loves the land "in spite of"—in spite of endless toil, sweat, anxiety, and backache it causes him owing to weed, insect, lack of nutrients, flood, and drought.

But the truth we learn from the garden is that if it is to be abundant, it needs some of this kind of faithful "in spite of" devotion. Gardens do not do very well if the gardener is away at the shore for four weeks. On return, many a gardener has been reduced to tears by parched and withered tomatoes, weed-choked beets and carrots, and aphids happily clustered undisturbed on the Brussels sprouts. An abundant healthy patch demands attention, devotion, and love.

The demands gardening makes on us often test our love affair with it. Often our problem in gardening as well everywhere else in life is that we love very poorly, at least to the degree Hosea describes. We love because it gives us pleasure. "I like your garden, but oh how I love the flavor of your tomatoes!" We love, not the soil, but our successes, our ability to grow things, touting our green thumbs about the neighborhood with baskets of succulent strawberries and snap peas, which isn't very far from our motivations in the rest of life. We work, sometimes hating what we do, but loving the ability it gives us to buy and possess certain fashions, things, badges of our accomplishments. We love others for what they can do for us, rather than for who they are and for what we can do for them.

But we mustn't be unfair in all this. As humans, we love imperfectly. We love what touches that indefinable something within ourselves that pleases us, or creates a certain well-being and contentment. We are naturally attracted to pleasing persons and attitudes. We are like the small boy who was asked what his favorite vegetable was. He said, "The pumpkin."

"Why the pumpkin?" came the perplexed reply.

"Because it smiles a lot," said the boy.

This isn't all bad, of course; it just falls short of a love that tolerates *un*pleasantness, or *un*lovable people with disagreeable attitudes—a love that calls us to inspirational sacrifice and hardship. It probably isn't too much to

say that without a few brief shining moments of Hosea's unconditional faithfulness here and there along the human journey, we might not have come so far as we have. In fact, even the briefest appearance of this sort of love defines us as human—created in the image of God.
Anthropologists talk of the evolution of humans going back millions of years. In 1978 Mary Leakey discovered human-like footprints in Kenya that were judged to have been made 3.7 million years ago. Yet the question that seems to survive an answer in all these bits of fossil evidence is, When did a *human being* actually emerge? Fossil jaws, skulls, footprints, molecular protein studies, carbon dating: none of this evidence can posibly tell us when—within this primitive skull—self-awareness emerged. Or, a step higher yet, when the brain cells and chemistry—long lost to dust under the cranial cavity—first produced logic and creativity. Or, still a step higher, when a being first became human in the image of God; that is, when that being voluntarily endured some hardship for the sake of a brother or sister or for some high ideal or principle without any intention of personal gain. When that first mighty heroic act of love took place, the first Adam emerged in one brilliant moment of history, and no paleoanthropologist will ever be able to tell us when that happened. It is that incredible act of voluntary hardship for the sake of another that connects us to God and pronounces us human; and if it did not happen somewhere in the past this would still be an animal world, and if it does not happen more often in the future this may be no world at all.
Agape[1]—unconditional goodwill, divine love, charity, whatever it is called—is a voluntary willingness to make unrewarded sacrifice for someone or for some good purpose and is the backbone and sinew of our humanity.

Without at least some moments, some brief flashes, some glorious interludes of this kind of love, our civilization would crumble and life would end.

One of the most startling claims Jesus made for himself he gave to his disciples just before his own death. It appeared that his dreams for the kingdom of God had become a feeble hope. His closest friends repeatedly misunderstood him and needed his constant correction. As he reached for the noblest and most audacious purpose in all of human history—to redeem the lost—they continued to be preoccupied with their own importance and their own place in glory. He faced a ruinous end, a mockery of his purpose and his claim for himself, a most agonizing death. Yet he had the *chutzpa* to gather his band about him in the last days of his life before the cross and say to them: "Apart from me you can do nothing" (John 15:5). It must have entered the heads of some that apart from him, they were at least making a living! Before they met him, they were managing to go about their business, maybe not with a whole lot of success, but at least they were surviving! Now, just when he'd gotten them in this mess and all seemed to be ending in disaster, he was telling them he was the source of their success? "Apart from me you wouldn't have been able to achieve anything. Apart from me there will be no future for you or the human race!" What Jesus must have meant was that without some of his unconditional loving in our lives we aren't going to make it. "Apart from my kind of love, you're going to fail miserably as human beings."

"This is my commandment, that you love one another as I have loved you. Greater love has no man than this, that a man lay down his life for his friends" (John 15:12-13). Apart from that you have no future.

Recent news articles tell us that scientists have

discovered a particle that, like glue, holds together the centers of atoms. They have appropriately named this particle a *gluon*. Apparently, physicists have never been able to completely explain what the elementary particles of the atom, like protons and neutrons, were made up of, except to theorize that there were even tinier bits and fragments of the atom to be discovered. But if every proton, for instance, were made up of smaller particles, what held them together? What kept them from flying apart? Well, the scientific community is ecstatic because a new accelerator has helped it discover the gluon, a basic ingredient of matter that holds it together. Taking a clue from the material world, can we conclude that there is also a spiritual ingredient that holds our emotional world together, keeping it too from flying apart? To sort of paraphrase Paul, If there is a physical glue, then there is also a spiritual glue. Love is the gluon of life, and God is love.

Whether our planet survives the next decade, or orbits the sun as a misshapen cinder for the next five billion years, depends on the amount of this gluon of life called love that can be experienced in our world. So too everywhere. Even in the details of life this gluon holds it together. No relationship (or connection) will last without it. Sometimes, someone has to make a sacrifice and do what is best for the other person in spite of the personal cost, or there is bound to be deadlock, pain, and eventual death—whether that relationship is between parent and child, husband and wife, labor and management, teacher and student, or one nation and another. First, someone must occasionally say, "Yes, I will grant you this advantage even though it will cost me or inconvenience me." It is a matter of survival. We need enough of the kind of love that bears the pain of relationships if our world is to stay together and not self-destruct by means of its greed, envy, pride, and selfishness.

Which is why, like gardening, this love has to do with the day-to-day particulars of life. Someone has said, "In order to be a true gardener you have to like to pull weeds." This love occurs in the daily attention paid to details. It has to do with putting the kids to bed, concern for the arrogant welfare recipient, understanding the disgruntled employee or employer, tolerating the unjust criticism, interceding for the helpless victims of the economy or prejudice or selfishness. It has to do with patience, sympathy, goodwill, kindness. It has to do with the everyday now we live in.

But it isn't easy. Most seem to be unable to love this way. There may be some well-adjusted people reading this, who by their own natural instincts remain constantly generous and sensitive to the needs of others, who are man enough or woman enough to bear the pains of life and still add love as it is needed. These people may skip to the next chapter, but the rest of us should not. When someone hurts us, we get ready to hurt back. When someone cuts us off in traffic, we would like to get out at the next stoplight and let the air out of that driver's tires. When we get taken, we plot how to take the next guy. For the rest of us normal people who are caught up in the materialism of our culture, who at times don't want to be nice to anyone, who sometimes even surprise ourselves with our insensitivity and anger—we need this gluon of life to hold our world together. And the only hope we have of finding it is through our relationship with God. Jesus spoke the point when he said, "Apart from me you can do nothing." His gluon becomes the wellspring from which we all must draw. Perhaps to learn how to love this way we need to declare a truce of God with all the wars we fight inside and outside ourselves.

Historians tell us that in Normandy when warriors and knights roamed the land, the only salvation for the common folk was the "truce of God." Fighting was almost a daily occurrence, prompted by petty neighborhood disputes between local barons. Often the countryside between castles in their undefended state became the victim of knights who could do pretty much as they pleased to the poor peasant and his crops, riding in full armor through the fields, fighting with other knights, destroying the gardens that kept the local people from starvation. Then the church came up with an idea. Realizing that they could never keep men from fighting, they declared

> the remarkable concept known as the truce of God, by which wars were forbidden in Lent and on certain saints' days and also every week from Wednesday evening to Monday morning. During these times peasants could warily till their field three days in the week and rest undisturbed on Sundays, but they were wise to take cover on Mondays, Tuesdays, and Wednesdays, when knights might come thundering through the crops intent on their quest for glory.[2]

Well, of course, this strikes us as a very humorous situation until we look at ourselves and see that we too fight without ceasing—even if the fields of our conflict are limited to doing battle with our own compulsive shortness of temper, relentless pride, senseless greed.

Should we not also declare a truce of God in the conflict? Today, this time I will not act as I usually do; instead, I will declare a truce with myself, invite God into the moment, and learn to love as he would have me do. Who knows, perhaps the idea would catch on in all the homes and villages, in all the factories and offices, in all the council chambers and legislatures, in all the capitals and summit meetings in the world. This time we will declare a truce and act as God would have us act and be and do this beautiful Godlike thing to one another to the glory of God.

And so the lesson from the garden is clear: Without at least some unconditional love, such as Hosea's, life will falter, and wither.

Gardening Note

In the garden some things die in order that others may live more abundantly. This process is called composting. It produces the best and cheapest fertilizer possible for growing things. Nearly every gardening book will give the author's personal formula for creating compost. Some are very elaborate with carefully constructed boxes and pens for the ingredients; others are quite simple without much fuss. The method best for each individual depends on how much effort the gardener is willing to devote to this worthy cause, the materials available, and the amount of time he or she is willing to wait until the finished product is ready to use.

The easiest way to compost takes the most time. One gardener devised about the simplest method of any. In the spring he set aside an area about six by twenty feet. On one end of the plot (six by ten feet), he started building a pile. First he added straw, leaves, and grass about six inches deep. Then from the other end he dug out some soil to sprinkle over the organic material already assembled. Throughout the growing and harvesting season he added chopped pea vines, cabbage stalks, carrot tops, kitchen scraps. After each new layer added, he dug more earth out of the unused end of the rectangle to cover. Occasionally he threw in a shovelful of lime, especially if he used leaves for any of the layers. He did this until frost. The pile just rested all winter. No turning. No special manures or proteins added to enhance the decomposition of the ingredients. This multilayered pile just sat.

In the spring, as if by magic his sandwich of earth and refuse had turned into rich, odor-free humus, which he quickly used up in preparing his garden for growth.

Then he began again, except this time at the end of the plot not layered before. To this new collection of organic debris, he added soil dug from the area where the earlier pile had been built. This worked fine for a few years until he had a hole so deep he could have built a swimming pool.

The lesson: There is no easy composting method. Like everything else in the garden, it takes work. The point should not be lost on us, however; when it comes to composting, nothing goes to waste in the garden. Even what dies remains a gift for the living.

5

ABUNDANCE AND EXTRAVAGANCE

My cup overflows.   —Psalm 23:5

There seems to be a common passion among gardeners. Without shame they brag about the abundance of their patch, gloating over their neighbor's insufficiencies and late-coming produce. Their gardens need to be prolific and first.

In a small New Jersey town, the friendship of two hobbyists got strained every summer when they competed for the first or biggest tomato. For years the semi–good-natured contest raged back and forth. First one displayed the earliest, or the biggest, or the most, then the other. One year, on the fourth of July, one of the combatants produced a fully vine-ripened tomato earlier than ever before—and surely earlier than his opponent. With a deceptive generosity he had the tomato gift wrapped and delivered by messenger to his neighbor's door. The recipient's wife has said her husband would not eat his supper that night, nor touch that tomato.

To get even, a month after the humiliating gift was delivered, the mortified man invited his gloating friend and his wife to his home for a late supper. Carefully waiting for the evening shadows to vanish into dusk, and after a couple of drinks, the host took his guest to the edge of his garden. He casually announced he had grown a tomato bigger than anything yet to be seen. They peered together in the dim light through the vines at a tomato the size of a cantaloupe. He begn to describe how he had methodically built up the soil back in November, adding rich humus. In the spring he obtained some well-rotted manure and worked it carefully into the earth. He took soil samples to be sure the nitrogen didn't get excessive, a problem that would produce lush vines but little fruit. He painted a marvelous achievement of forethought and agricultural technology—and all went well until an unexpected breeze came up. The covetous visitor noticed the tomato move rather peculiarly. Getting closer he saw through his friend's game. He had blown up a red balloon and attached it to a vine, counting on the dim light to obscure his deception. It is said the friendship did not survive the strain of that night.

Morton Hunt, in his *New York Times* article " 'Deadly Sins' of an Unrepentant Vegetable Gardener,"[1] confesses to the same depravities revealed by these two warring neighbors. With a shameless hardness of heart, he writes,

> The most despicable form my pride takes is publicly topping others' efforts at vegetable gardening. Ah, the warm glow I feel when a dear friend comes for drinks or dinner and remarks disconsolately that my tomatoes are ripening earlier than his, my bean vines are lusher, my broccoli bigger, my squash more abundant! What joy to assert my superiority in the guise of self-deprecation. Sometimes I manage to display my gardening potency by bringing in an overflowing basketful—seemingly by chance—just when visitors are on hand. You might say

I'm a Foodstuff Flasher. What a boon! How many chances does a chap have to display his potency in public without being arrested?

Gardens as viewed by tillers of the soil can never be overly prolific. Extravagant rewards from gardening seem to touch off an insatiable madness to produce even more—the perfect head of Boston lettuce, or a cabbage worthy of slaw for a month, or cauliflower as huge and white as a snowdrift. Gardening can become addictive and hazardous to your health, once the notion of vegetable power hits the backyard turf. The gardener can be seen mainlining seed catalogs in January in order to keep his or her habit going until spring. This person can become intoxicated with the idea that his or her family and a good share of the neighborhood can become self-sufficient to the point they may never darken the aisle of another freezer or produce counter again. This person can get hooked on omnipotence over the soil, believing in the magic of his or her own green thumb.

Yet even though nature often conspires to keep the gardener's pride in check, through horticultural diseases, insects, pests, drought, floods, and other agricultural catastrophies, if the truth be known, even the most brazen, overbearing, and successful gardener is a mere trifle in the scheme of creation. Whether the gardener admits it or not, his or her efforts are fourth class to what really makes it possible—the incredible propagation of life. Living things possess a distinct tenacity, which often hides the ineptitude of the home gardener. Even in the desert there is life; it can be seen by turning over rocks and scrutinizing the sand intensely. The ice caps produce oil! Once at least, even in these barren frozen wastes, life teemed, to one day produce fossil fuel for our technological compulsions. Life wants abundance. It seems bent on producing more than necessary. It displays a certain extravagance without which the gardener's efforts would be reduced to futility.

A certain gardener is said to count completely on nature's resolve to grow things; she neither tills nor fertilizes. Each year in a heavily mulched area she merely sows seeds and waits for them to grow to picking time. This may be one of those questionable stories that appear occasionally in popular gardening magazines to harass the poor man who still does it the hard way and spades his garden, but it does make the point that the combination of seed and soil are *meant* to grow things. Life is meant to multiply. Growth is durable and abundantly prolific. It will not be stopped.

The persistence of growth can be seen in New York, not far from the Hudson River's Bear Mountain Bridge, on the Appalachian Trail. There, a tree grows with a stone as big as a football in its trunk. The sapling must have found root in a rocky wall that had been thrown together by farmers a hundred years ago. As it grew it fought against a stone above. Incredibly, it grew around it on both sides, gradually lifting the stone in its trunk four feet in the air!

Someone grew tired of the growth of randomly windsown trees behind his garage. Besides, they shaded his garden. He cut them all down leaving the stumps protruding a foot above the gound. Now he has an uglier and more dense growth than he started with. *All* the stumps sprouted an abundance of shoots that have reached ten feet in the air within a year's time!

And who hasn't dug grass or weed or flower out of a crack in the asphalt driveway? Often digging out isn't enough. Chemicals need to be found to pour into the crevice to discourage growth once and for all.

Some gardeners imagine at the peak of the season they can hear their gardens grow, and they step carefully through them in order to stay out of their way and avoid encirclement by their vines! Life is abundant indeed, and there is a built-in positive growth force in nature before which the gardeners for all their bragging must be humble. So that as they look out over their pea patch, they can wholeheartedly say with the psalmist that it is the Lord who prepares a table before them in the presence of the enemies that would defeat them, whether they be wind or rain or pest or predator or drought or their own ineptitude. Gardeners can feel the wonder of God's fecundity by allowing themselves some honest moments while hoeing the rows.

All of this raises an interesting theory—could it be the Lord had to resort to an extravagance in life in order to make creation stick? Is this why in the beginning he set loose on the earth teeming varieties of species and commanded, "Be fruitful and multiply"? Is this why the Old Testament so often speaks of the shame of barrenness, since the empty womb was a symbol of opposition to God's intentions? The Lord fired a shotgun filled with the pellets of life expecting one or two to hit the target and grow and multiply and survive. So seeds are sown by the hundreds in order to produce a few trees, or sperm enter the womb by the thousands in order for one to find its way up the fallopian tube to fertilize a solitary egg, or hundreds of bits of pollen cling to the hundreds of hairs on the body of a bee in order to produce a single apple. Creation is an extravagant gesture with a bias toward life. Even physicians who battle disease, in their most philosophical moments, see the inherent predisposition of humankind to align itself with survival. Lewis Thomas, the writer-physician, says of the variety of life called *Homo sapiens* that it is "amazingly tough and durable" and remarks that the natural tendency of the human body is toward health.

But quite possibly the prolificacy of creation became necessary because of all that opposes survival. Paul, acutely aware of all that discourages life and growth, writes that "Creation itself [is in] bondage to decay. . . . [and] has been groaning in travail" (Rom. 8:21, 22), so that in the beginning it *was* necessary to set loose a multitude of spores and pollens and sperm and eggs in order to make the bias persist. Even the cosmos seems to oppose life. In all the solar system and as far as is known by searching with radio telescopes far into the silences of space, no other life exists. Some scientists are of the opinion we are alone among all the suns and galaxies in the cosmos. That is a forlorn, solitary thought, but also one that tells us how difficult and rare it was for life to get started on our special planet. It is no wonder Christians believe it took a deliberate act to get it going, and now many Christians believe it will take a deliberate act to keep it going through a wholehearted return to Christ's way. Survival in this atomic age still requires a lavish expenditure, which explains the extravagance of Christ. Christ is God's survival system. Christ is God's mark on all the history of our planet. Christ is God's intention that life, growth, maturity, and survival will take place in spite of the dis-ease that surrounds us.

Is there any doubt Jesus' life was an extravagant gesture? Was it not a wildly wonderful, reckless thing to do to allow the very soul of life to be born to an obscure family in a hostile culture in a poor and forsaken corner of the world? Bethlehem is more daring than creation itself. *And expensive:* The most glorious, loving, hope-filled, sensitive, challenging, insightful personality of all times was executed to end a short thirty-three years on earth.

Abundance and Extravagance —— 63

And reckless: God expected humankind to get the message after Christ's death, leaving it to a handful of confused men who had all the human failings of pride, envy, fear, and insecurity. *And prolific:* The words, deeds, and stories illumine the human character and condition in such a way that the richest and poorest of human minds and souls have been unable to avoid his influence; thousands upon thousands of men and women have been caught in the fascination of his presence.

So it is little wonder that our Lord, himself, reflected the Father's extravagance. Jesus often used high-toned language. He exceeded expected limits in order to make a point. It was not unusual for his hearers to respond to him with, "Wow! Who was that?"

Prayer, he said, could move a mountain and cast it into the sea.

Sin, rooted in human nature, was so heinous and deadly that if the eye be the cause, better to pluck it out and throw it away; if the hand, better to cut it off.

He shocked from their complacency people who satisfied themselves with "I do the best I can" religion. He told them their righteousness must exceed the purest among them: "You, therefore, must be perfect, as your heavenly Father is perfect."

Over and over again he revealed an accepting, inclusive Father who far exceeded the narrow limits presumed by those who thought themselves the favored ones.

He deeply disturbed the faithful and satisfied elder son, who witnessed the biggest party the homestead had ever experienced when his rowdy younger brother returned home to his bed and board.

He startled the go-getters, the successful, and the winners by telling them that the poor, the meek, and the afflicted people had already been blessed by God.

The union boss's ears sharpened immediately when he described God as the employer who gave every worker the same amount of money regardless of how many hours of work appeared on the time clock.

Everywhere he carried the message of God's grace and love in vivid displays of wonder.

He told of a God who is willing to leave all the faithful in pursuit of one lost soul. He included in his kingdom all who turn to him in spite of what they have been, and he was willing to risk all his energies, even his life, for the crumbs of humankind. He knew, as Paul Scherer has so beautifully stated it, the extravagance of love: "Love is a spendthrift, leaves the arithmetic at home, is always 'in the red.' And God is love."[2] In Jesus' kingdom the surprising enormousness of the love of God becomes evident with the inclusion of the excluded. Brother Lawrence knew the surplus of the Lord's love when he joyfully found himself surrounded with the best gifts the kingdom had to offer. He considered himself

> the most wretched of men, full of sores and corruption, and who has committed all sorts of crimes against his King. Touched with sensible regret ... I ask His forgiveness.... The King, full of mercy and goodness, very far from chastising me, embraces me with love, makes me eat at His table, serves me with His own hands, gives me the key to His treasures; He converses and delights Himself with me incessantly, in a thousand and a thousand ways, and treats me in all respects as His favorite.[3]

Jesus knew the Father's penchant for extravagance, so his word was like a hammer chipping away the complacency and dullness of his listeners.

The Word of God is prolific, extravagant with gift and love, with an intense bias toward life and maturity and growth in *creation* or *salvation*. Soil and wind and rain and blossom and fruit, or speech and deed and tenderness and forgiveness and truth; God's way is the way of abundant life indeed!

It is a profoundly humbling and joyful experience to discover we are the undeserved recipients of such extravagance, yet so many people seem to lack the organs of sight and sound that track, locate, and listen to such abundance, which is why God overreacts to get anywhere. Which is why Jesus described the found Kingdom with a certain exuberance—as banquet, treasure, party, celebration, joy. At an immensely gifted time, if anyone should get within hearing distance of the "party," the response they are almost compelled to make is unmitigated, unashamed ecstasy. Which leaves those who do not hear the joy in great wonder.

It is rather like an incident that occurred in a New York bank as reported, again, in *The New York Times:*

> There a woman whose head was bracketed by earphones delighted the lineup with her dancing. That she was obviously unaware of the audience made the performance even more delightful.
>
> She wore a red jacket and blue jeans and was featuring a wicked hip motion—half twist, half stripper. She kept her forearms high, fists clenched and knees loose. Her feet favored front-to-back, rather than side-to-side—not easy when your hips are working in counterpoint, and once in a while she did a kind of dip, and smiled. The rest of the time her face was a mask of concentration.
>
> Pausing only for the minutes it took to cash her check,

she left the way she came—dancing and dipping, leaving her watchers to wonder whose music was responsible for this magic.[4]

Christian joy can also leave others wondering whose music is responsible for the magic. In that we have received a gift so generous, costly, and lavish, it is hardly possible to resist a "performance more delightful" than the melody of God's extravagant acceptance. Surely it is a gesture that weaves its way through all of life and is essential to our survival.

Gardening Note

The tomato is the most prolific of garden vegetables, with the exception of zucchini. However, the tomato inflicts a cruel irony on the gardener so that one wonders it is grown at all with any affection. For nine months of the year (depending on where one lives of course), the vegetable lover suffers with cellophane-boxed tomatoes from the supermarket. All that time the home gardener's mouth dreams of eating *one* solitary vine-ripened tomato still warm from the sun, juice running down the cheeks, the flavor sensuously confirming belief in heaven. Yet in spite of everyone's longings, the tomato stubbornly refuses to submit to any attempts to reproduce its unique mid-summer flavor artificially. On or around the celebration of the American Independence, however, the tomato vine plays its malicious trick and like the sorcerer's apprentice will not stop producing an onslaught of the most delicious varieties imaginable. The vine becomes so prolific that the gardener's spouse and neighbors lock their doors against the fecund invasion and the generosity of a grower desperately seeking an outlet for the wildly productive vines. The tomato turns on and overpowers its loving benefactor, taxing all ingenuity to dispose of it usefully and creatively.

But take heart! Here are some possibilities: First, eat them! This will surely test one's digestive capabilities, but the experience of justifiable gluttony can be exhilarating when the vine-ripened tomato is the tempter into sin. Besides, one may be inventive in the process and try every conceivable way a tomato may be devoured. The experience might even lead to a classic cookbook on varieties of tomato consumption. One innovative gardener swears to the ambrosia of his tomato sherbet.

Second, give them away. Although precisely when you have them to give, so does everyone else. But it is well to persist. It could happen; by a stroke of good luck the gardener could find a family that hates gardening. If this should occur, giving tomatoes away can bestow subtle joys on the giver, such as a certain altruistic feeling, which can do wonders for bad moods and rainy days. And who knows, the recipient may feel a genuine obligation to pay off the debt some time later!

Third, can them. There is absolutely nothing new about this gambit except that also there is nothing so beautiful in January as to open the cupboard and see the neat rows of glistening red jars, which contain at least a hint of the richness of July and August. The penalty, of course, is the necessity of enduring steaming caldrons and kettles in the canning process during the worst heat of the summer. One can escape the sweat by freezing, but freezing make tomatoes watery and far less tasty then the old-fashioned canning method.

Finally, tomatoes can be dried. In fact, sun-dried tomatos are considered a luxury. Northern Italy produces most of our imports, which are packed in olive oil and sold in gourmet specialty shops.

Although you do not need an electric home-style fruit dryer to dry tomatoes, it is considerably easier than actually sun-drying, in which you must contend with flies and other insects, and the sudden appearance of clouds that diminish the sunlight.

Plum tomatoes of the Italian variety are best to use since they contain less juice and more pulp. Simply split them in half, squeezing gently to expel the seeds. Place in the dryer for about one hour skin-side down, about two hours skin-side up. Some juices will be retained.

Pack a clean, sterilized jar with the tomatoes. Pour enough olive oil to cover. Seal. They can remain in the refrigerator until ready for use. When tomatoes are removed, add a little olive oil to keep those covered that remain. Sometimes, including a fresh bay leaf adds a little variety.

This is one more way of happily managing the tomato invasion and skillfully dealing with its spiteful joke.

6

BREAD FOR THE WORLD

If a brother or sister is . . . in lack of daily food, and one of you says to them, "Go in peace, be warmed and filled," without giving them the things needed for the body, what does it profit?
—James 2:15-16

Three gentleman gardeners of sorts gathered themselves in the shade of a backyard apple tree to sip a late afternoon drink. Some mild-mannered comparisons had been made about one anothers' successes—actually the third man delicately announced that he was not big on gardening if it required a person to break into a sweat. He casually reflected on his style of husbandry when he said, "The best way to get real enjoyment out of the garden is to find a nice shady spot under a tree, pour yourself an iced tea, and happily watch your neighbor perspire in the sun hoeing his beans. And, if you appeal to his green thumb vanity, he'll probably give you his surplus so you can savor 'garden fresh' at the dinner table without lifting a finger."

So the conversation went, each according to his own intensity of fervor agreeing that there were limits to one's energies when it came to tilling the soil. One of the more enthusiastic admitted, "I love to work in my garden, but I wouldn't want to do it for a living."

To which the other enthusiast replied, "Yeah, I agree. I don't garden because I need the stuff to eat. I need it for a nice therapeutic escape. When the grandchildren arrive I have a reason to get out of the house. I forget most of my troubles when I'm a little sweaty getting some dirt under my fingernails." Crop raising as a necessity, they all agreed, had to be tough.

Most people when they try to cultivate their first pea patch start out with visions of vegetables the likeness of January's seed catalogs. It all seems so easy. With plenty of advice from the neighbors, with hoes and rakes and packets of seeds (or seeds conveniently arranged in plantable strips of tape), black plastic, fertilizer, and watering can, they attack the most likely spot on their acreage. They dig and rake and remove the biggest stones, put in some fertilizer, make little rows, plant the seed, and moisten the soil. Soon they are eating radishes, lettuce, and green onions, and it is all so easy they wonder why anyone should be hungry. But then, of course, June moves into July and the sun bakes the earth dry, weeds seem unconquerable, disease and insects nearly kill off the tomatoes, cucumbers, and cabbage, the rabbits eat the broccoli, and neophyte gardeners wish they never started. They keep accounts and, adding up receipts for hoses, tools, fencing, fertilizer, black plastic, screening, wheelbarrow, seeds, and a freezer to winter over the crops, discover that their tomatoes cost $5 each. Even if gardeners decided to buy produce at a farm stand at top dollar and take the advice of a wise man about where to *hire* a gardener to make the place presentable, they would come out ahead financially and be saved a whole lot of anxiety and backache as well. Even for the serious gardener, it has to be hard work, disappointment, and at least in the beginning, expensive. So if in addition, whether you eat or not depends on the success of your gardening skills and the weather and how hungry the predators are around the neighborhood, you've got a whole lot to worry about. If even with all the advantages of modern farming it's tough, what must it be like when the water supply is unpredictable, no fertilizers are available, the soil is too sandy, and there are no garden centers or agricultural agencies to get advice from about insecticides, soil erosion, and chemistry? If even with all the resources we fail, how do they make it in some countries where few of the conditions are right?

The point is, you can't be a gardener without some second thoughts about how difficult it must be in less fertile and resourceful countries. If you are at all in touch with the world's food problems, you can't help feeling a little guilty about going into a rage when the rabbits eat a few beans. To us, beans are a hobby, to much of the world beans are the difference between life and death. The three men under the tree discussing the virtues of gardening, who felt just a little uneasy when they speculated how it must be to *really* depend on what they grew, hardly touched on the real truth about American gardens.

In most of America, we lose perspective about hunger, real need, and poverty. We are like the fisherman who kisses his wife and goes off in the morning on a party boat with a six-pack of beer to catch some big fish for the freezer. Getting nothing after spending all that money for the equipment and boat, he can't face his wife empty-handed, so he stops at the fish market on the way home to buy just enough to convince her the adventure was worthwhile and he should go again. In most other countries there is no fish market to stop at, and even if there were there would be no money to buy the fish, so there wouldn't be much to eat until the fisherman tried again the next day. Most people in America don't understand the anxiety of deprivation, hunger, and want. Our anxieties have to do with how much our share will be of the good life. Our married children often become distressed if they can't find an affordable house in a nice neighborhood big enough to hold all their wedding presents. We have taught them high-minded tastes and expensive goals, and often those first years on their own they feel deprived because they have to live in a three-room apartment without air-conditioning, near a bus stop on a busy highway, twenty miles from the job. We panic over burned toast in the morning, a stuffy office to work in during the day, and a clogged filter in the swimming pool at night.

We are like the man out in a boat one hundred yards from the shore who decides to swim to the dock, but he misjudges the distance and his swimming abilities and twenty yards from shore panics because he is out of breath and strength to go any farther. He flaps and screams and founders only to suddenly discover he is in three feet of water. Most of our complaints and hardships are in three feet of water, where much of the rest of the world is in over their head.

A newspaper article describes the misplaced anxiety at a local garden center. It is reported when the owner arrives to open up in the morning people are already waiting, holding bags and cans containing bits and pieces of their sick lawns and ready for him to sell them a cure. Some become hysterical when he pronounces their lawn dead. Of all the suburban symbols of the good life, lawn is supreme. "People are spending more and more time and money on their lawns every year, most of it on front lawns" says one garden center proprietor. A university study estimates that about $200 million a year is spent on Long Island lawns alone. At many home gatherings and cocktail parties it isn't unusual to hear heated discussions about whether it's best to water early in the morning or late at night, or whether grass clippings are good or bad for the lawn. Talk about dethatching, aerating, liming, weed killers, and turf builders becomes serious and obsessive, and when the "lawn doctor" pronounces their sod beyond help, sometimes people cry. It is hard with that kind of consciousness to understand hunger and deprivation at emergency levels in much of the world.

We simply do not understand how privileged and rich we are in America. In a news article the United Nations reported that seventeen million children around the world died from hunger and disease in 1981. Even more tragic, UNICEF said the deaths could have been prevented at the cost of under $100 a child. "Far from being priceless, a child's life was worth less than $100 in 1981," says an executive for the fund for children. "Wisely spent on each of the poorest 500 million mothers and young children in the world, such a sum could have bought improved diets and safer sanitation and more water, the basics of life." The $200 million of fertilizer dumped on Long Island lawns would have saved two million children. How then do we justify our anxieties about dandelions in the lawn, overcooking the filet mignon, and losing our prized lettuce to the summer heat?

But what in good conscience are we to do? Writhe and beat our breasts in guilt over our priorities and anxieties over verdant gardens and patios? Hunger is an issue that needs to be settled among nations. We can invoke God's wrath against those countries who ignore human suffering as does the psalmist:

> Now therefore, O kings, be wise;
> be warned, O rulers of the earth.
> Serve the Lord with fear,
> with trembling kiss his feet,
> lest he be angry, and you perish in the way;
> for his wrath is quickly kindled.
> (Ps. 2:10-12)

Besides calling down the heavens on indifferent politicians, we in America can vote for the most hunger-conscious officials. We can support organizations that care: Bread for the World, CROP, World Vision, and others. But what are we to do about our own consciences when we haul food we really don't need into our kitchens and freezers just because we enjoy the garden?

We can give the produce away. One woman decided to give away her entire week's crops at the peak of August harvest. She brought three bushel baskets filled with tomatoes, beans, zucchini, eggplant, and cucumbers and spread the produce out on a long table at a local bridge tournament. Before she had hardly displayed her goods, one of the wealthiest quickly gathered up the best of the harvest and stored it in the trunk of her limousine.

We could ship it to the poor. Hardly. Produce is the most perishable of foods, and who would distribute it? A "system" would need to be devised. Someone would need to be hired to supervise the project. Clerks would need to keep accounts so no single family receive more than other families. "Poor" would need to be defined. Distributors might skim off the best before it got to the hungriest. Where would the money come from to cover expenses? Another bureaucracy would be created to eat away and betray another high purpose.[1]

We could give it up. Stop growing things. Let the

ground return to weeds, or seed it with grass and aside from keeping it cut, let nature take its course. It would save us backache, sweat, anxiety, and a guilty conscience. But how does that saying go? "To go through life without a bumper sticker, is to have no opinion at all." Well, if we are *for* food for the world we can hardly be *against* gardens; we have to take a stand and grow things.

There is a line from Psalm 104 that helps. After listing all that the Lord has done in his creation; that is, bringing forth food from the earth, and wine to gladden the heart of man, oil to make his face shine, planting the cedars of Lebanon, giving the moon to mark the seasons, feeding the young lions, and bringing forth the sea filled with teeming things, the psalmist gets completely carried away with his reflections and in ecstatic joy lifts his hands to the heavens and says, "Thou renewest the face of the ground" (Ps. 104:30). God is able to send forth his Spirit so that the very essence of his creation is renewed. Even the patches of earth that refuse the seed its growth? Even the human heart empty and arid of compassion? Even the conscience-stricken gardener who reaps abundance in a land already overgrown with plenty? Yes, even the very ground of our being that he has exposed to pestilence and greed and guilt. Even *that* ground he is capable of renewing. God is intimately involved with his creation and is still able to change the character of soil and soul. When the Spirit is in the heart of the gardner something happens, another level of awareness emerges, something new begins when a person puts his or her work into the earth. The consciousness of the planter becomes more acute about the hungry; but more so, the work itself becomes a means of glorifying God.

For one thing, the soil itself becomes an immense gift. The feel and smell of it in the springtime speaks of its rich potential for life. It teems with possibilities in every corner of the earth. When the Jews took over the deserts from the people who had wandered the arid wastes for centuries, they promptly learned how to grow things. Even the poorest soil is a gift. The land is like the soul. If you neglect it, leave it to itself, it will grow weeds, or worse, become inhospitable and wasted. So too the human soul. Neglected, it has the terrible capacity to subvert and exhaust itself. But God can renew the face of the ground or soul, depending on the receptivity of the gardener. This seed, this digging in, this cultivation, this weeding and harvesting and sharing is all gift and all to God's glory. Teilhard de Chardin, a priest but also a scientist respected by the best in his field of anthropology, wrote, "God is not far away from us . . . he awaits us every instant in our action, in the work of the moment. There is a sense in which he is at the tip of my pen, my spade, my brush, my needle—of my heart and of my thought." Work without God has the capacity to become drudgery; work in the presence of God has the power to become the peace of God.

Nicholas Berdyaev said, "Bread for myself is a material question, but bread for my brother is a spiritual question." When we dig and plant and consume with all the earth's family in mind, *that* sweat and lumbar pain is spiritual and in a sense an invitation for all the people of the world to do the same because our work becomes our prayer. And that prayer is the hope that in all the world the poorest and loneliest will be fed.

A rather obscure Old Testament story of David (II Sam. 9) has some power to it. David and Jonathan's friendship is legendary. But Jonathan, along with his father, King Saul, has died in a terrible battle with the Philistines at Gilboa. When a survivor of the battle tells David about

Jonathan's tragic death, his grief overwhelms him. Later, David seeks to honor his relationship to Jonathan and asks one of Saul's servants if anyone remains in the former king's household. Yes, one poor soul still lives, Mephibosheth, Jonathan's crippled son. A blemished son? He had to be the most neglected of men, in a land where physical flawlessness was deemed necessary in service to God. Yet David, out of sympathy for his friendship, calls Mephibosheth before him. Jonathan's son with no self-esteem prostrates himself at David's feet, describing himself as a "dead dog." David raises him up and gives him all that belonged to his grandfather—his lands, possessions, and his servants. But then with a stroke of genius for symbolic and poignant action so charcteristic of David, he proclaims that for the remainder of Mephibosheth's life, a place will be made at his table for him to eat. "So Mephibosheth ate at David's table, like one of the king's sons" (II Sam. 9:11). David included at his table the poorest and most forsaken of men, and we must do as well for all the Mephibosheths of this world, to the glory of God. We must do so by raising the consciousness of nations *and* by the symbolic dedication to God of our work in the garden patch.

It is no little thing, this sort of symbolism. Jesus was well aware of the power behind such actions: "On the night when he was betrayed [he] took bread" (I Cor. 11:23). For thousands of years, that act has been repeated at the Lord's table. We need to remind ourselves that as we daily eat, we eat at God's table because it is his creation and we are invited to do so. We need to see every scrap of food produced as a family table that stretches across the whole wide world; and as long as the faithful remain the King's guests, no wounded heart, no poor soul, no starving human being need be completely lost ever again.

We are descendants of Mephibosheth. Aware or unaware of it, we've been eating a the King's table as one of his sons or daughters, and all that is brought to that table belongs to the world; all the little prayers and dedications and moments of praise and hymns and harvests and work and battles to get things to grow—all of it accumulates to feed the whole earth and give it life.

Gardening Note

If our spot of ground, our sweat, our harvest is to be a symbol of God's abundant grace capable of renewing the soil and soul, then that symbolism ought to be worked out in ways more obvious than the obscure meanings of our religious convictions.

So as a gardening note of some substance, here is a list of agencies concerned about world hunger. Along with the January seed catalog, why not also write for a "catalog" from one of the following. Better yet, why not send an amount equal to what we save on our gardening to our favorite anti-hunger organization?

American Friends Service Committee
1501 Cherry St.
Philadelphia, PA 19102

American Jewish Joint Distribution Committee
60 E. 42nd St., Rm. 1914
New York, NY 10165

Baptist World Relief, Baptist World Alliance
1628 16th St., N.W.
Washington, DC 20009

Bread for the World
802 Rhode Island Ave., N.E.
Washington, DC 20018

CARE
660 First Ave.
New York, NY 10016

Catholic Relief Services
1011 First Ave.
New York, NY 10022

Christian Reformed World Relief Committee
2850 Kalamazoo Ave., S.E.
Grand Rapids, MI 49508

Church World Service
475 Riverside Dr.
New York, NY 10115

CROP
P.O. Box 968
Elkhart, IN 46515

Lutheran World Relief
360 Park Ave., S.
New York, NY 10010

Mennonite Central Committee
21 S. 12th St.
Akron, PA 17501

National Council of Churches Task
  Force on World Hunger
475 Riverside Dr.
New York, NY 10115

Oxfam-America
115 Broadway
Boston, MA 02116

Salvation Army
799 Bloomfield Ave.
Verona, NJ 07044

Task Force on World Hunger
Presbyterian Church (USA)
341 Ponce de Leon Ave., N.E.
Atlanta, GA 30365

United States Committee for UNICEF
331 E. 38th St.
New York, NY 10016

World Bank
1818 H. St., N.W.
Washington, DC 20006

World Council of Churches
   Commission on the Churches
   Participation in Development
150 Route de Ferney
1211 Geneva 20, Switzerland

World Vision
919 W. Huntington Dr.
Monrovia, CA 91016

7

WINTER

Thou hast fixed all the bounds of the earth; thou hast made summer and winter. —Psalm 74:17

A television commercial shows the snow swirling through the kitchen door and a seven-year-old stomping in from the weather and with a look of despair, heaving a great sigh to his beleaguered mother and saying, "I need it bad." The pitch is to encourage the viewer to escape the cold with a trip to Florida, Aruba, or the Bahamas. This bit of doggerel usually appears on the tube after the harsh reality of winter has set in, so most who watch the video scenes of tropical serenity are already sick of weather that stalls traffic, delays trains and buses, and transforms gutters and sidewalks into floating slush ponds. We presumably all "need it bad"—escape from winter. Yet that commercial fails to ring true. No seven-year-old wants to get away from the snow, which often keeps him or her out of school and provides great adventure at the same time. If the child does, he or she suffers a severe handicap; adulthood at seven could cause permanent disfigurement. But so too can the seriousness of being an adult at any age. It is the child within us that rejoices over the snow even as it threatens to undo our plans and obligations. It is through the eyes of the little girl or boy in us that we are able to see the wonderland that emerges after a rain has frozen on the trees, even when the commerce of daily traffic is paralyzed by ice-bound roads. (We can still imagine, in spite of age, the exhilaration of sliding joyfully across a frozen sidewalk!) And, in the beginning of our faith journey, it is the child in us that sees God and believes. So possibly, it is our lost child that keeps us from liking winter. Our inability to accept the frost and cold says something to us about our inward condition.

More than in anyone else, a child dwells in the personality of every successful gardener. The digging and planting and picking all "hook the child," which is confirmed by the witness of sprouting things emerging from milk cartons in nearly every kindergarten or nursery school as spring approaches. Thomas Harris describes the child in adult personalities. He says children experience the firsts in life with a grand *a-ha*.[1] The first stroking of a soft kitten, the first drinking from a garden hose, the first submarine chase with a bar of soap. In every gardener that same *a-ha* is experienced as she reaches into the vine and finds the first sun-warmed, vine-ripened tomato, or the sudden appearance of a glorious yellow star on the zucchini vine, or the first strawberries in the springtime. Gardeners, have no fear. Your positive, happy child is well and alive!

Gardeners do have mixed feelings about winter, however; mostly because they do not want the growing period to end. Great pains are taken to be prepared to withstand the first frost. Perishables like tomatoes, peppers, cucumbers, and beans all need to be picked before freezing temperatures descend on the patch. The ideal is to let them continue to grow right up to the eve of the frost, so it is not unusual for a late-night weather report to send the gardener hurrying out to the backyard with flashlight in hand to pick the remaining fruit, cover plants against the cold, close the cold frame, and move potted flowers indoors. The coming cold seems to bring with it a certain heroism. Every gardener, as winter threatens, feels part of a desperate fight to keep life going as long as possible. In the fall at least, if you are a gardener it's hard to bring yourself completely around to the winter-loving point of view.

So there may be times in a gardner's life when people who actually prefer the cold are incomprehensible. A man remarked that he preferred winter because he could always add clothing to keep warm, but in the summer there was a limit to what he could take off to stay cool. He had one of those mind-over-matter bumper stickers that said, "Think Snow." Sometimes it is hard to withstand a rising suspicion about people who flap their arms and dance up and down to keep warm in the snow while raving about its beauty. People who like the cold have to be viewed with a critical eye. Richard Adams, in his book *Watership Down,* has the rabbit's-eye view of such overexuberance about the frost: "Many human beings say that they enjoy the winter, but what they really enjoy is feeling proof against it. For them there is no winter food problem. They have fires and warm clothes. The winter cannot hurt them and therefore increases their sense of clearness and security. For birds and animals, as for poor men, winter is another matter."[2] Possibly some people are so insulated against the winter they hardly know its cruelties. The changes it brings do not affect them. The thermostat, the heated garage, the down jacket and insulated boots, the apartment that requires no shoveling, the public transportation that does not depend on batteries being thawed—all these except in the most severe circumstances keep them from the real changes winter brings. There is no similar escape for the gardener.

Winter is a reality that can't be avoided. Winter is cruel and beautiful at the same time.

So the true gardener learns to beware of the frost and appreciate the winter. The child within wants to play it both ways—keep things growing and enjoy the snow. So he or she accepts it both ways and allows winter to teach. The gardener learns to speak zucchini and to listen to winter.

Winter reminds the gardener, for one thing, of what a novelty a garden really is, because most of creation takes on the character of winter. Untenantable surroundings are never far from us. Fred Hoyle, the British scientist, reminds us that lifeless outer space isn't remote at all: "It is only an hour's drive away if your car could go straight up." So too, just a few Fahrenheit degrees one way or the other is a matter of life or death for many growing things. The earth's tilt of a few degrees on its axis, which creates the seasons, is the margin for survival. A severe drought can cause deserts to form and entire cultures to disappear beneath the sand. If it rains too much, vegetation may choke out the light, and darkness kill off the sun-loving varieties of life. A slight rise in the average polar temperature could send melting ice and floods into temperate climates killing and disrupting civilization. A shift in the jet stream can bring uncommon storms to beaches and drive fish south or north out of their normal habitations and ruin local fishermen. Even in the beginning of creation we are told small differences in the cosmic drama could have prevented life. Science laureate Robert Jastrow says, "In a dozen different ways, you find that the smallest change in the conditions of the universe would have made it impossible for life or man to be here." We plant and cultivate in a narrow row of hospitality. When all these variables are considered, life is privilege, boon, gift, favor, miracle.

So songs sung among the beans and corn should not be cause for surprise. By a whole series of miracles, the pot boils to receive the plenty from the patch that touches the taste buds with fresh-picked flavors. It is the fact of winter, indeed the bleakness and inhospitable nature of nature— the great cosmic winter—that makes the bean row speak so eloquently of God. We live in a rare window, possibly a unique window, of survival where all the necessities for life are given to us in a very tiny space in the infinite universe. The garden is a clue to God's grace. As Paul says, "Ever since the creation of the world his invisible nature, namely, his eternal power and deity, has been clearly perceived in the things that have been made" (Rom. 1:20). Surely, "his invisible nature" can be perceived in the pea patch when frost hardens the ground. How, in all the forbidding cosmos, has this tender-leafed lettuce come about? What hand has set aside the exact condition for the tomato to ripen, the corn to sweeten, humankind to flourish? Creation is grace. When we hoe the row, how can we be anything but grateful for the change, and praise God for the plants? Winter is never far from us.

Yet another word that comes to the home grower out of listening to the winter is that it is necessary. Winter is sabbath for the pea patch and pea picker alike—a resting time. Gardens need time to be dormant. Like people, they cannot keep producing without time to regroup, replenish, and ready themselves for the next push to bear fruit. In the fall the land is cleared of weeds and vegetation, the pH is checked and lime added as necessary. Compost, manure, or peat is dug into the soil to increase its organic content. The snow comes to gradually leach moisture down into the humus and lime to blend it into a growing medium that vegetables in particular adore. The gardener too needs rest from all the hoeing, weeding, planting, and picking. Winters are given to us so that we can adjust to the changes we have come to expect, and to bring us hope of blossoms and growth and green again. There are reasons for the methodical progression of seasons. We all need once in a while, along with the team that loses the World Series, to be able to say, "Wait until next year!" We need fresh starts and new opportunities. We need to experience the process of expectation again and somehow understand that because we've goofed things today, tomorrow still holds the possibility of allowing us to play in a completely different ballgame.

Actually it is only in rest that we escape for a time the winter winds that seek to chill our summertimes. God has given humankind the great gift of contemplation. Here, even in winter, we are able to call into our consciousness sunfilled beaches, hot sand underfoot, children at play in the surf. We can visit again faraway places, see their dullness or beauty, the details of a building's bricks or a street's wet pavement after a summer shower. We can experience emotions again, feeling the joy of a sunset or the awe of a canyon. This sabbath is meant for such contemplations where at best we can recall—relive—our loftiest moments. Our mountain tops can be had again, and we can be reminded of God's faithfulness to bring the promised springtime.

Joseph Bayly, in his book on the Christian view of death, *The View from a Hearse*,[3] tells how on a cold January morning he ran from his house in shirtsleeves to get the mail in the box by the road. As he quickly glanced through the postman's leavings, the freezing wind blowing the snow about his feet, he saw he had a Burpee seed catalog.

On the front were bright zinnias. I turned it over. On the back large tomatoes. For a few moments I was oblivious to the cold, delivered from it. I leafed through the catalog tasting corn and cucumbers, smelling roses. I saw the freshly plowed earth, smelled it, let it run through my fingers. For those brief moments, I was living in the springtime and summer, winter past.

Bayly says likewise as Christians we always have the gift of recalling the eternal spring during the winter seasons of life because we have Jesus Christ. So too in any winter, it is a blessed sabbath for the gardener when he or she can contemplate the soil and seed and crop and in the wonder of it all praise God for the assurance of another harvest, yet another springtime of heart and soil.

So we are reminded that what we see is not all there is to be seen. The sabbath-winter calls us to remember the seed beneath the snow. All it takes is some imagination—vision!—to see the fruit again. Someone has said "Happiness is a form of courage." So too, happiness is a form of imagination. When winter descends on a life, imagination is required if there be any hope for the springtime. The winter comes to sharpen our creative visions of brighter things and happier times. Except for the earth's shielding of the sun we would not see the stars. So, too, the drab mid-winter coaxes us to lift our sights to warmer horizons, yet unseen and unlived.

In the Christian life this is part of the Spirit's work. Except for the Spirit we would be overwhelmed in our winters. One can't help reflecting on the Pentecost experience (Acts 2), when the disheveled disciples and believers gathered aimlessly together in a bewildered fashion asking, "Well, brothers and sisters, where do we go from here?" After all, the future didn't look like much.

The excitement of the Resurrection had died down. Those who gathered together had lost their leadership. The only authority they had was a reluctant Peter, who up to then was clearly unsure of himself. The Jewish and Roman officials still searched the streets for those who had been Jesus' friends. Certainly it was a winter season filled with indecisiveness, nervous waiting, nondirection. Fear and misunderstanding had descended on the faithful. An indifferent observer would have judged that the future for this group huddled together in Jerusalem wasn't very promising. There was nothing to indicate they would be in any way successful, let alone grow and expand their mission. With a little negative encouragement they might have gone back to their fishing, tax collecting, wool gathering—except that the Spirit interceded. Out of the whirlwind the message came to them that things might look cold and unpromising, but things are not always what you think they are. There appeared to them a dimension they hadn't taken into account.

Pentecost reassures us that life is not what appears in front of us, but contains another reality that once encountered can be of greater substance than even the frost-hardened ground. Again, Paul Scherer speaks of an ingredient that has the capacity to make life understandable: God's own Holy Spirit. "Our life shows too many symptoms of another life that impinges on it, presses against it from every side, rattles the shutters it tries to close, knocks at its doors, and turns the knob. We are impossible conundrums without it, answerless riddles."[4]

For Christians, God is the warm springtime breeze that has a potential for bringing forth blossoms in the winters of life, which we need to keep in mind, because mostly what we hear of—wars and crimes and brutalities—shocks us into despair. But an intangible, unpredictable, invigorating, divine disturbance moves through and allows us to see with new eyes and listen with new ears so that winter in the foreground merges to spring and summer in the background.

If we listen, though, winter teaches us another thing. Winter is part of the process. Life is not winter. Life is winter *and* summer. "While the earth remains," the Lord promised Noah, "seedtime and harvest, cold and heat, summer and winter, day and night, shall not cease" (Gen. 8:22). We need to be reminded continually when winter comes that it is only *interlude,* a necessary step toward blossom and fruit.

A travel bureau once promoted its steamship cruises with the slogan "getting there is half the fun." For certain impatient gardeners whose vision seems locked into bushel baskets of produce being lugged into the kitchen, "getting there" isn't half as much fun as the harvest. But winter slows us down and helps us consider the journey. Possibly one of the biggest struggles in the Christian life is to change from goal-oriented person to a journey-oriented person. Most often we are goal-oriented people. We dream of making the touchdown, the match point, the home run. We are winners, goal setters, and we rejoice in success, achievement, and reward. But Jesus held that instead of the goal, the journey was sacred. He said, "I am the *way.*" The early church, recognizing this world as part of the process, called themselves women and men of the Way—wayfarers for Christ. They were journeyers for God, pilgrims, people who knew the value in the process of getting there.

And there is great value in being a journeyer. For one thing, a journeyer is less likely to get upset when the drive toward the goal is interrupted. Have you noticed? We get frustrated and anxious when we have some specific goal in mind and are intently moving toward it, and the phone rings or someone drops in for a chat. If we are extremely goal conscious, we find it very hard to tolerate intrusions. Have you ever had your plans interrupted by someone who just goes on and on about something that seems to you has nothing to do with anything very important? And, you keep saying to yourself, Why doesn't he leave? or, Doesn't she have anything better to do?

Gardeners should learn to savor every stage in the progress to harvest—the rich, moisture-laden earth freshly tilled in the springtime; seed and sprout in orderly rows; thinning and watching for insects; mulching and hoeing; gathering and picking; clearing and liming; shredding and composting—all stages worthy of living in. Such gardeners will not lose soul to a crop that fails owing to storm or rain or cold or pest.

The more we become journeyers, the more we will see the value in the things that happen to us on the trip, and the fewer anxieties we will have over the interruptions and delays. The more we become journeyers, the more alive we'll be because we'll begin to see the intrusions as an important part of life, to be cherished as much as our achievements; more so perhaps, because they are life's way of breathing into our souls the thought that our own importance is overrated, and that the things we imagine we have to accomplish do not give us nearly the joy or the satisfactions we suppose.

As Christians we ought to consider seriously that the journey *itself* is the goal. This may not be such a radical thought. George Bernard Shaw wrote, "I dread success. To have succeeded is to have finished one's business on earth, like the male spider who is killed by the female the moment he has succeeded in his courtship. I like a stage of continual becoming, with a goal in front and not behind."

We should think of ourselves as becomers—constantly moving toward the prize but appreciating the journey; like the man flapping his arms in joy as the snow swirled around him. After all, we live in the moment, not in some future time. This cup of coffee we are drinking or preparing, how can we love the person who shares it with us or for whom we prepare it? This moment in worship, how can we let God seep down into our bones and flesh and mind so that we can make this time so special we carry his presence into the rest of the day or week? These people we meet who all have needs and hurts and joys just as we do, how can we live better through our encounters with them, even come to cherish their companionship and the example of their faith? This way that we travel, how can we increase the quality and value of every moment? How can we better enlighten the journey with the insight of Christ, with him as companion? Are we people of the Way? Or, are we single-minded, straight-line personalities who have our eyes so riveted on a goal that we miss the fun in getting there?

Another thing about winter: It teaches us to wait. In winter the soil waits for the spring to stir. Isaiah promises that

> They who wait for the Lord shall renew their strength,
>   they shall mount up with wings like eagles,
> they shall run and not be weary,
>   they shall walk and not faint.   (Isa. 40:31)

Strength comes out of waiting—for winter to pass.

We live in a land that hates to wait. In foreign countries waiting becomes routine. Long lines form to get a bit of gristly meat. You must wait at restaurants to be served, wait in the long lines for the bus or tram to come, wait for your baggage to arrive; but here in America we have speed checkout counters at the supermarket, fast food restaurants, instant breakfast drinks and food processors to chop, mash, slice, blend, and shred in seconds. We do not like to play the waiting game. Gardeners find that they are no exception, waiting for the first vine-ripened tomato, for the zucchini to blossom, the corn to mature, the lettuce to sweeten; it all seems interminable. But again, Isaiah claims waiting gives us strength.

The strength comes through humility and waiting teaches humility. It takes the starch out of our pride. To wait unnoticed on a bench at a restaurant while satisfied people file out the door helps rid us of the "I'm in charge" or "I'm important" complex. Waiting is a perfecting process that cleanses us from haste, agitation, impatience, and pressure. That is, if we wait long enough. If we get into the habit of waiting (dare it be suggested we deliberately choose the *longest* line at the checkout counter, and take the *most* congested road to work!), our countenance may gradually change to patience and peace.

And, prayer is waiting. Waiting for the spirit to be moved. Waiting to hear something from the Lord. Waiting for his presence. Waiting for the wandering thoughts, the cold feeling, the boredom, the fear, the impatience to pass into God's rest.

So winter and waiting are not all bad. It is rather like Frederick W. Farber wrote: "We must wait for God, long, meekly, in the wind and wet, in the thunder and lightning, in the cold and dark. Wait and he will come," because the springtime promises us that.

Gardening Note

Henry C. Harris had been a backyard gardener all his life. Because he had the soil in his blood and under his fingernails, he resented winter. He swore to his wife they would someday move to Florida or California where he could grow things year-round.

This particular winter seemed especially cruel to Henry. The first hard frost was the earliest on record. Caught unprepared, he lost his green tomatoes and lingering peppers. The ground had become stone-hard and remained impenetrable for months. The ground became so inhospitable it would not even receive a corpse. Cemeteries were backlogged.

Yet a peculiar thing happened in Henry's garden. One cold day as he walked the dog near the place where his tomatoes grew only a few months before, he saw something green emerging through the inch or so of light snow that had fallen in the night. He couldn't believe his eyes. On hands and knees he brushed snow away to discover a spot of earth that had remained soft, fertile, hospitable to seed. A tomato plant had come to life in January!

How could he explain it? Why had this particular spot of ground remained soft? What mysterious power had been so determined to maintain life in spite of frost and winter?

He had no idea. But he ran to the back door to call his wife. The dog, sensing excitement, began to bark. His longtime friend and neighbor took notice and came to see. Henry showed them his discovery, joyfully predicting the end of winter, the chance to work the soil year-round; by some miracle his patch could become fertile again. All he had to do was discover the mysterious reason this particular spot had spawned growth. He excitedly announced to his skeptical wife and his troubled neighbor the greening of the winter!

Yet Henry noticed his friend's sadness and became resentful. "You are envious of my discovery. You are not happy for me. You, I thought to be a friend, I have discovered to be just another jealous neighbor. Anyone can cry with a man's disappointment, pain, or tragedy, but it takes a real friend to rejoice at a man's success, achievements, and rewards."

Henry's neighbor looked shocked. No, it wasn't envy or jealousy. Henry had misread him. If this discovery were true, if all that Henry had claimed came to fruition—gardening year-round—his thought ran to sadness because he had learned to love the winter, the quiet beauty of the snow. He'd discovered winter to be more transparent than all the other seasons and therefore more understandable. He could see things through the trees that the summer foliage hid from his eyes. He loved the silence of the cold nights, with moon and stars the only visible signs of warmth. He loved the sabbath from his gardening chores. Winter was a time of reflection that, having given him the opposite side of the coin to summer, had helped him appreciate the gentle, greening earth in the spring.

Turning to Henry he said, "Do you suppose the earth needs to remain silent for a time in order to live again? Just as we humans need to remain silent before God in order to hear him and so also live again? What would it be like to never experience another springtime? Where would we get the joyful anticipation and inspiration of the rebirth of things? How would nature ever remind us of its overt partiality for life? Where would we find the pull of God's creation toward its creator? Who or what would ever care again about the greening of our souls?"

As he listened, Henry's eyes filled with tears. He knew his neighbor's love for the soil, and he knew he spoke the truth.

While his wife watched, as the neighbor slowly departed, he pulled up the sprout. With his boot, he pushed the snow over the place where the earth remained soft. Gathering his wife's arm to himself, he slowly made his way with her for the warmth of home.

8

THE PARABLE OF THE SOILS

A sower went out to sow.   —*Matthew 13:3*

That same day Jesus went out of the house and sat beside the sea. And great crowds gathered about him, so that he got into a boat and sat there; and the whole crowd stood on the beach. And he told them many things in parables, saying: "A sower went out to sow. And as he sowed, some seeds fell along the path, and the birds came and devoured them. Other seeds fell on rocky ground, where they had not much soil, and immediately they sprang up, since they had no depth of soil, but when the sun rose they were scorched; and since they had no root they withered away. Other seeds fell upon thorns, and the thorns grew up and choked them. Other seeds fell on good soil and brought forth grain, some a hundredfold, some sixty, some thirty. He who has ears, let him hear."

(Matt. 13:1-9)

Whoever the sower is, he is not a very good farmer! If he be God, then he is true to form, scattering seeds helter-skelter in all directions, not caring where they land. True to form so it seems, grace being what it is—unpredictable, easily declined, given to the most unlikely people. No farmer would be so wasteful with good seed. Especially a farmer in Jesus' day who had no Burpee catalog to rely on, but with great care had to preserve his best varieties from year to year. Also, no farmer would sow the seed on any soil not already prepared to receive it. The farmer would have plowed, removed the rocks, put in the manure, and harrowed the soil before sowing.

But that God is not such a good farmer isn't so shocking. The first *Homo sapiens* were not hunters for nothing—all they could find to eat in God's garden were a few berries and fiddleheads. Who wouldn't prefer hamburger! Then there is that old story of the man visited on his farm by his pastor, who sanctimoniously reminded the hardworking sodbuster how marvelously good of God it was to provide so much abundance. To which the farmer respectfully responded, "Well, preacher, it might be as you say, but you should have seen my fields when God was tending them all by himself!" So God provides the system; it's up to humankind to make the system work.

But obviously God isn't worried about his image; he's much more concerned about the condition of the soils—the receptivity of men and women. Judged from a distance, the parable is a warning to those who would treat God's grace lightly, brush it off as nothing, place higher value on other things. He is saying you will never enter the Kingdom until you do something about the condition of your soil. "Get with it," Jesus is saying. "Do what is required to allow the seed to grow and bear fruit. Learn the language of the kingdom of righteousness and make it work, spring to life, bear fruit a hundredfold."

Later Paul would write, "Work out your own salvation with fear and trembling; for God is at work in you, both to will and to work for his good pleasure" (Phil. 2:12-13).

Exactly! God casts his seed into every human heart; in one form or another he is ready to work in everyone. Yet it is a small seed, so it should be guarded with apprehension and trepidation. It will need much care and tenderness to grow to fruition.

In the spring when the first seedlings are put outside, great forethought must be given them. Danger from frost must be minimal. Because of their tiny root systems they must not be allowed to dry out. In some cases a cutworm collar needs to be placed around the plant to keep this voracious caterpillar from clipping the young stalk off at ground level. A period of hardening is often required; time to allow the plant to adjust from a heated greenhouse to cool nights. The farmer does what is needed in order to bring the garden to fruit. Likewise the human soul.

People ask, How do I get faith? The answer is, Do what needs to be done. Prepare the soil for the seed. Go to worship. Take time every day to pray. Meditate on some incident in the Gospels. Picture what it might have been like to have sat at table with Jesus—the texture of his robe, the dirt under his fingernails, the dimness of the candlelight, and the flickering shadows on his face. Read the Scriptures—repeat the same psalm every day for a month. Prepare the soil!

Behavioral psychologists have a saying: "Get in motion and you'll get the *e*motion." If you are feeling negative, lethargic, indifferent, then to feel otherwise you need to start acting different from the way you feel. Force yourself to get up on time. Take an interest in something or someone. Go for energetic walks, expose yourself to people. If you keep it up long enough you'll begin to feel different. You'll get the *e*motion. The seeds of hope, joy, purpose, and self-acceptance that want to grow inside you will flourish—thirtyfold, sixty, a hundredfold.

Mostly we'd prefer miracle to hard work. It would be much nicer if gardens bearing beans and tomatoes and corn suddenly appeared overnight like Jack's beanstalk. It would be nice if one morning all the stars had arranged themselves in the night over our pillows and we awoke free of despair, helplessness, and self-pity. It would be nice if we could walk into church once, or pick up a Bible, or hear a radio preacher, and become Mother Teresa at the twinkling of an eye. It would be nice, but excluding very rare exceptions the seed doesn't grow that way.

Elie Wiesel tells the story of the Hasidic Master of Kotzk who listened with some impatience to a complaining disciple: " 'Look, [Rabbi]! God created the universe in six days—and it's ugly!' 'Would you have done better?' snapped [the rabbi]. 'Eh, I think so,' stammered the forlorn disciple. 'Yes?' shouted the Kotzker [rabbi]. 'Then what are you waiting for? Start working—right now!' "[1]

And we need to start with that single bit of God's creation we can actually do something about—our own poor soils. We need to learn how to be consistently prepared for grace and lead receptive lives like the praying Muslim whose upturned hands are ready to catch every seed wildly sown from heaven.

Not to be avoided, however, is the plain harsh truth that the parable ponders the particularly stubborn mystery of the human soul. Its infertility to heaven's generosity. Reading the story in Matthew, Jesus seems to be looking into the faces of those in the crowd and brooding about what it really takes to bring his human part of the Father's creation to fruition. For the most part it is as if they lack some nutrient. Their soil is too acidic and inhospitable; the seed simply will not germinate. Jesus must have spent considerable time pondering this puzzle. Several parables deal with it, chief of which are the story of the rejected banquet and the story of the soils. In fact, the story of the soils is followed by a somewhat bewildering dialogue between Jesus and his friends wherein the Lord reminds them that this mystery is centuries old because the prophet Isaiah considered the same when he said,

> You shall indeed hear but never understand,
> and you shall indeed see but never perceive.
> For this people's heart has grown dull,
> and their ears are heavy of hearing,
> and their eyes they have closed. (Matt. 13:10-17, 34, 35)

What an enigma this monotony of ear and eye and heart and soul!

Yet it is still true that we know more about soils than we do about souls. We know how to make the "desert . . . blossom as the rose" (Isa. 35:1 KJV). We know the nutrients required to make things grow. We can chemically analyze the earth, study plants, experiment with growing conditions, regulate water supplies, and grow tomatoes in the arctic and strawberries at the equator. But we cannot *make* a person hear the truth, reorganize priorities, or know God. Shortly after the first moon landing, *The New York Times* editorialized:

> For all his resplendent glory as he steps forth on another planet, man is till a pathetic creature, able to master outer space and yet unable to conquer his inner self; able to conquer new worlds, yet unable to live in peace on this one; able to create miracles of science, and yet unable properly to house and clothe and feed all his fellow men; able eventually to colonize an alien and hostile environment and yet increasingly unable to come to terms with the nurturing environment that is his home.[2]

So, one thousand nine hundred and sixty-nine years after Jesus spoke his parable, the same mystery flourished and flourishes. And now, an even more disheartening question looms before us. The mystery has led us to ask, Will the soil of this earth called humanity ever be fertile and receptive enough to produce the fruits of good will, empathy, and peace in time to save the planet? The shadow that is cast over that question by the parable is that *some* soils will never grow anything. It is an unsettling idea that some people are beyond grace, yet Jesus seems to be saying, "Yup, some people will never understand or bear fruit."

One gardener reported that he had planted parsnip seeds in a newly dug area in his backyard. He loved parsnips. He loved going out the following spring when the first thaw was then allowing him to dig them out. It was as if in the cold something lay hidden and alive and fruitful; even their sweetness increased through the hardship of winter. But the seeds had never germinated. He went out and bought new seed and double-sowed them; they still didn't come up. For some reason, in that soil, parsnips would not germinate. Are some people like that? Will the Spirit of God never germinate in the soil of their lives? Will they never know God? Are they beyond grace, help, redemption, rehabilitation?

A pastor once told the story of how his suburban church sought to redeem troubled kids in the neighborhood. They gathered a board of directors: school psychologists, representatives from the local mental health center, teachers, influential community business people, police officers, social workers. They hired an experienced youth counselor. On certain evenings of the week, they opened their church hall. They put out the word this center was for everybody. They especially wanted troubled kids. They got troubled kids, who broke up the furniture, punched holes in the walls, smashed windows, and drove the hired expert counselor to more fertile ground. At least once, the church called the police to investigate some unusually destructive vandalism. The officer in charge was not sympathetic. He blamed high-minded church officials. He claimed the night the center was open, troubles increased throughout the town. He said, "These kids are beyond help! They even bite the hand that feeds them. Even my dog doesn't do that! You think you're going to help them; the only thing to do is put them in jail and throw away the key!"

Was he right? Were these soils incapable of growth? Were they like Humpty-Dumpty in that all the psychologists, social workers, churches, and clergy couldn't put their lives back together again? The pastor of that church said with all his heart he wanted to believe that police captain wrong.

And yet Jesus says some soils are hardened, rocky, filled with weeds; and the dark truth glares at us out of the gospel pages that even the most loving, Spirit-filled, magnificent human being failed to inspire some soils to growth. In fact quite unexpectedly, he inspired them to commit the most monstrous evil in history; they convicted him, cursed him, betrayed him, misunderstood him, and nailed him to the cross. Even Christ himself couldn't reach some people. So possibly the police captain is right. We should throw away the key, give up expecting poor soils to grow anything worthwhile. We should forget some people who are beyond even the power of the Almighty to change. Is that so?

No! We shouldn't give up on anyone. *True,* some people are beyond redemption as difficult as that is to say, but it is not given to *us* to know who they are. We may in our judgment give up on someone, only to discover later this person has, by some divine gift of tragedy or hardship or success, become a new person. The Romans raised three crosses on Calvary hill. One held the Christ, the Son of God. The other two held criminals. They, by the Roman justice of the time, deserved to be there. They were throw-away men. Cruel men. Roman law judged that society would be better off without them. Yet at the last moment, one turned to Jesus asking for mercy. The other died cursing God; for him the seed fell on hardened ground. For the one seeking mercy, some tiny seed had been sown, who knows how many years before, had surprisingly sprouted, taken form, and now the man was reaching in one glorious terrifying moment for heaven.

Time and time again we Christians especially are prone to write off someone. We judge that person lost, too far gone, too arrogant or superficial or selfish. But that is our limited judgment. Years later we meet the same person and find that the soil of life he or she has lived in has transformed the person. It is not given to us to know how God will work among the ignorant, arrogant, indifferent, callous, busy people who so often disillusion us. God's vineyard is full of miracles. Miracles that we too often casually dismiss or fail to consider. Which accounts for Jesus' optimism. Jesus knew the power of miracle.

Surely one of the most optimistic announcements Jesus ever made is found in the Parable of the Soils. He began his story quite simply, yet it is these first few words that tell us volumes about Jesus' hope. We can picture him standing by the shore looking inland as the crowd begins to gather in front of him. Being pressed on all sides, nearly pushed into the sea, he gets into a small boat and sits in the bow a few yards from the shore; and he begins to teach them, and says, "A sower went out to sow." In those six words Jesus gives us hope and optimism about the future. True, much of what follows in his story is negative. Some seeds fall along the hardened path and birds eat them. Some fall among rocks where the soil is too thin to sustain them. Some fall among thorns and weeds where they are choked off. But then some fall on good soil, which brings "forth grain, some a hundredfold, some sixty, some thirty." In spite of the fact that some seed is lost, still, a "sower went out to sow." Did a farmer ever sow without expecting a crop? Was there ever a pessimistic farmer in the springtime? If a man sows, he must be hopeful there will be a future harvest, mustn't he?

Sometimes people get into those periods when the days ahead are uncertain. It may be surgery, an unknown diagnosis, a sudden illness. The best thing to do at such times is to go out and sow a future. Plant some tomatoes if the season is right, fully expecting to taste their vine-ripened elegance in a few months. Buy a series of opera tickets extending into next year, anticipating the romantic beauty of a Puccini or Verdi aria. Invest some money in a thirty-month Certificate of Deposit, counting on collecting the best interest rate available. In faith, do something with some future in it, like Jesus' words "a sower went out to sow"; it will do marvels for a person's outlook and energy for the days ahead.

Jesus, picturing the sower, sees God, who is not discouraged about a future harvest even when the elements might be working against him. Even though the weeds and rain and drought and birds and predators seek to deny him a crop, the sower goes out to sow, completely sure about receiving abundant fruit from the labor. Even though there are some who will not, or cannot, go below the surface of the world's hype and glamour and easy words or principles, even though there are those who are intent on squeezing every possible joy and privilege from life to enhance their own pleasure, even though the horizon looks dark with the tumult of hysterical men who threaten to destroy the harvest forever, the sower goes out to sow expecting a future. The sower *expects* a good soil. The sower rejoices to see the soil that responds to the gift of every seed cast upon it. That is, all human beings who cling to the best that is within them and who rejoice when the best is seen in others, every person who would deal with another with honesty and generosity, every fertile soil that, in spite of what life appears to give, is able to rejoice at seeing more than the obvious, all hearts that beat to the music that by their own careful listening is heard above the raucous cacophony of the deadly rhythm of life, all believing soils, that hearing the voice of Christ gladly claim him as their own, humbled by the miracle of their own hearing, forever rejoicing in the generosity of a God who wants to include them in his household—in such as these do the seeds find hope of germination and harvest, some a hundredfold, some sixty, some thirty.

In a powerfully symbolic way, gardeners represent people who believe in the future, which is not a bad thing to do in today's world, where even those who claim to be part of the harvest predict doom and chaos in the days immediately ahead. This parable needs to be bound back to back with all the biblical prophecies of apocalypse gleaned from Ezekiel, Daniel, and Revelation. This is a parable of cautious optimism in spite of the stark reality that many of the earth's soils will be arid and barren forever. This parable comes from the lips of him who knew he could not trust himself to even those who believed him, "Because he knew all men and needed no one to bear witness of man; for he himself knew what was in man" (John 2:23-25); yet, he was able to count on a future so much that he pictured it as if a farmer went forth to sow in the fields knowing the good harvest promised. It is the marvelous audacity of Jesus that is his great gift to us. Here he was facing arrogant, self-righteous men who largely controlled his own religious traditions—and these men hopelessly outnumbered him. Here he was facing the end of a nation he loved, seeing in its young sons and daughters its death throes because of their wildly zealous patriotism that would soon level Jerusalem and scatter his brothers and sisters for nearly two thousand years. Here he was almost standing alone; while he lived no one he could count on understood him. Here he was, loving the world, ready to forgive even while he knew what men had in their hearts to do to him. Here he was so sublime and loving ready to go all the way for a world that hardly deserved it, believing he was taking on himself all earthly misery and injustice and despair, trusting in the Father to make it right. What can we say of this incredible, courageous, confident Galilean except that his example of trust in the future so far exceeded that of even the most courageous of men that when we meditate on his life, words such as Lord, Savior, Emmanuel tumble from our lips. If Jesus trusted the future as much as that, should we not expect as much from the days ahead? Will not God still do the unexpected? Will he not still grow out of the good soil a marvelous hope? Will not his seed still come alive even when the winds and rains above it threaten to wash it away?

Dietrich Bonhoeffer, living in the hideous darkness of Hitler's Germany, jailed by the Nazis, wrote these words some months before his death by hanging:

> It is wiser to be pessimistic; it is a way of avoiding disappointment and ridicule, and so wise people condemn optimism. The essence of optimism is not its view of the

present, but the fact that it is the inspiration of life and hope when others give in; it enables a man to hold his head high when everything seems to be going wrong; it gives him strength to sustain reverses and yet to claim the future for himself instead of abandoning it to his opponent. It is true that there is a silly, cowardly kind of optimism, which we must condemn. But the optimism that is will for the future should never be despised, even if it is proved wrong a hundred times; it is health and vitality, and the sick man has no business to impugn it. There are people who regard it as frivolous, and some Christians think it impious for anyone to hope and prepare for a better earthly future. They think that the meaning of present events is chaos, disorder, and catastrophe; and in resignation or pious escapism they surrender all responsibility for reconstruction and for future generations. It may be that the day of judgment will dawn tomorrow; in that case, we shall gladly stop working for a better future. But not before.[3]

Bonhoeffer, receiving his trust in the future from his Lord, did not "abandon it to his opponent." Clearly the opponent of all that is holy is reflected in wars, hunger, injustice, deceit, threats of atomic incineration. We cannot abandon the future to such as these and pretend that somehow they are God's will. We must work patiently to bring about the business of the kingdom—love, joy, peace, patience, kindness, goodness, faithfulness, gentleness, self-control (Gal. 5:22-23). We are farmers, earth lovers, ever ready for seed to ripen in the good soil. We still hoe the row expecting a crop, and we praise God for the joy of every tomorrow.

Gardening Note

Paul writes, "But, you may ask, how are the dead raised? In what kind of body? How foolish! The seed you sow does not come to life unless it has first died; and what you sow is not the body that shall be, but a naked grain, perhaps of wheat, or of some other kind; and God clothes it with the body of his choice, each seed with its own particular body" (I Cor. 15:35-38 NEB).

The human body is as a seed; unless it be cast into the ground it cannot rise to life. Without seeds, there can be no life. We can imagine with Paul, God cherishing his seeds from season to season, knowing they will not all germinate, but knowing as well that those who do will complete their intended purpose. They will come to life, grow, flourish, and blossom with him forever.

So also, the seed in the planter's hand is cast into the ground in order to complete its intended purpose; to rise up and flourish and bear fruit. The gardener too recognizes how important it is to cherish the seeds, so they are saved from one planting to the next.

There is the story of a gardener who gave some tomato seeds to his neighbor. For the giver, he could not have offered a more cherished gift than those seeds, because they were part of a family legacy. His was the third generation that had carefully preserved this special variety from season to season. He had received them from his own deceased father, who had first taught him the love of gardening and the love of Christ. He said he often thought of his father as he saw these seeds grow to fruition. As the tomato grew ripe and red in the warmth of the summer sun, he visualized his father at that moment not needing sun or moon but immersed and ripening in the light of the glory of God (Rev. 21:23). Each year as he planted these seeds he reminded himself of the Resurrection. His father's seeds still lived.

But how best to preserve tomato seeds? Some have

reported their seeds saved from prior seasons have had poor germination records or have not come up at all.

Here is the best way to do it according to the experts. Select the best of fruit, free of blemishes, and allow it to ripen fully on the vine. Cut it open and scoop out the seeds (some pulp will remain attached), and put the seeds into a jar half filled with water. Allow this to remain several days at room temperature. Stir occasionally. Some seeds sink to the bottom. These are the ones to keep. Carefully remove them and allow to dry thoroughly on a paper towel. Seeds must be completely dry. Store in a tightly sealed container. The best place to keep them is a frost-free refrigerator. Seeds store best at cool temperatures. It is recommended, in order to be doubly sure of dryness, to add a couple of tablespoons of powdered milk secured in a facial tissue. This will gather up any random moisture from other refrigerator items.

One thing we can do as gardners is pass on our best seeds to our children and befriended gardeners as a legacy. They will be a reminder that as these seeds depend on the power of soil and nature to come to life, so we too have depended on the power of the Spirit of God to come to resurrected life.

NOTES

2. The Battle for Life

1. "The Strife Is O'er," *The Hymnbook* (Richmond: Presbyterian Church in the United States, 1955), p. 182.
2. "God, Who Touchest Earth with Beauty," *The Hymnbook* (Richmond: Presbyterian Church in the United States, 1955), p. 97. Copyright © Irwin Publishing Inc., of Richmond Hill, Ontario, and used by permission.
3. Annie Dillard, *A Pilgrim at Tinker Creek* (New York: Bantam Books, 1974), p. 92.
4. Carl Sagan, *Cosmos* (New York: Random House, 1980), p. 330.
5. From "Ash Wednesday" in *Collected Poems 1909-1962* by T. S. Eliot, copyright 1936 by Harcourt Brace Jovanovich, Inc.; copyright © 1963, 1964, T. S. Eliot. Reprinted by permission of the publisher. World rights by permission of Faber and Faber, Ltd.

3. Survival Language

1. Paul Scherer, *Love Is a Spendthrift* (New York: Bantam Books, 1972), p. 127.
2. *Harvard Magazine*.

4. Love It or Leave It

1. *Agape* is one of three Greek words translated into English as "love." Agape is used when John writes "God is love."
2. David Howarth, *1066: The Year of the Conquest* (New York: Harper & Row, Publishers, 1978), pp. 63-64.

5. Abundance and Extravagance

1. 24 July 1983. Copyright © 1983 by *The New York Times* Company. Reprinted by permission. 24 July 1983.

2. Scherer, *Love Is a Spendthrift*, p. 12.
3. Brother Lawrence, *The Practice of the Presence of God* (Old Tappan, N.J.: Fleming H. Revell Co., 1975), p. 36.
4. "Fast Shuffles Cashdance"—Editorial, *New York Times*, 14 August 1983. Copyright © 1983 by The New York Times Company. Reprinted by permission.

6. Bread for the World

1. *The Christian Century* of October 5, 1983, reported an incident where altruism met the relentless indifference of bureaucracy: "Harlan Yarke, a McHenry County, Illinois, dairy farmer, recently decided to give one day's milk from his cows to the poor. He asked his milk processor, the Oberweis Dairy Company, not to pay him for the milk but to process it and donate it to the poor people in Aurora. The Oberweis Dairy pasteurized the milk, put it in half-pint and half-gallon cartons and gave it to some church-sponsored charities. The donated milk cost Yarke about $120 in lost income. Two months later, the U.S. Department of Agriculture threatened to sue the dairy for not paying Yarke. The administrator said that under the federal milk price-support subsidy program, Oberweis broke the law in not paying Yarke for the milk, even if the farmer agreed to donate it. The administrator has referred the matter to Washington for adjudication." Copyright 1983 Christian Century Foundation. Reprinted by permission from the October 5, 1983, issue of *The Christian Century*.

7. Winter

1. Thomas Harris, *I'm OK—You're OK* (New York: Harper & Row, Publishers, 1967), p. 27.
2. Richard Adams, *Watership Down* (New York: Macmillan Publishing Co., 1972), p. 418.
3. Joseph Bayly, *The View from a Hearse* (Elgin, Ill.: David C. Cook Publishing Co., 1969), p. 94.
4. Paul Scherer, *For We Have This Treasure* (New York: Harper & Brothers, 1944), p. 16.

8. The Parable of the Soils

1. Eli Wiesel, *Somewhere a Master* (New York: Simon & Schuster, 1981), p. 110.
2. Editorial, *New York Times*, 1969.
3. Reprinted with permission of Macmillan Publishing Company from *Letters and Papers from Prison*, revised, enlarged edition by Dietrich Bonhoeffer. Copyright © 1953, 1967, 1971 by SCM Press, Ltd. World rights by permission of SCM Press, Ltd.